ROUTLEDGE LIBRARY EDITIONS:
POLITICAL THOUGHT AND
POLITICAL PHILOSOPHY

Volume 32

RETHINKING SOCIALISM

RETHINKING SOCIALISM
A Theory for a Better Practice

GAVIN KITCHING

Routledge
Taylor & Francis Group

LONDON AND NEW YORK

First published in 1983 by Methuen & Co. Ltd.

This edition first published in 2020
by Routledge
2 Park Square, Milton Park, Abingdon, Oxon OX14 4RN

and by Routledge
52 Vanderbilt Avenue, New York, NY 10017

Routledge is an imprint of the Taylor & Francis Group, an informa business

British Library Cataloguing in Publication Data
A catalogue record for this book is available from the British Library

ISBN: 978-0-367-21961-1 (Set)
ISBN: 978-0-429-35434-2 (Set) (ebk)
ISBN: 978-0-367-23365-5 (Volume 32) (hbk)
ISBN: 978-0-367-23370-9 (Volume 32) (pbk)
ISBN: 978-0-429-27955-3 (Volume 32) (ebk)

Publisher's Note
The publisher has gone to great lengths to ensure the quality of this reprint but points out that some imperfections in the original copies may be apparent.

Disclaimer
The publisher has made every effort to trace copyright holders and would welcome correspondence from those they have been unable to trace.

New Foreword (2019)

Rethinking Socialism was written in the immediate aftermath of the Conservative victory in the 1983 British General Election. It expressed my anger at the inability of the Labour Party, led by Neil Kinnock, to defeat what was (then) the most right-wing British government since the Second World War, despite that government having presided over a major economic recession which had left over 3 million people unemployed. It also expressed my conviction that the standard left-wing explanations for its defeat – the role of the 'reactionary' press in preventing the Left's message from 'getting across', the role of the Falkland's War in 'distracting' voters from the Thatcher government's domestic failures – were partial at best, and mere excuse-finding at worst.

I therefore set out, in the book, to analyse some more basic shortcomings of the British Labour Left in particular and of 'left-wing' radicalism in Britain generally. I argued that the most fundamental of these was a failure to understand contemporary capitalism – its economic dynamics and the complex moral and political problems they create for left-wing policies. Given this focus, the book was seen, by some of its reviewers at least, as a harbinger of the subsequent 'Blairite' takeover of the Labour Party and the embrace of 'neo-liberal' economic policies by the Labour governments of the 1990s.

However, to read *Rethinking Socialism* that way is to ignore one of its major themes – the ominous and ever-worsening competitive *failure* of capitalism in Britain. As I put it in the book's fifth chapter, since 1945 British managers had conspicuously failed to manage, to maintain or increase the national and international competitiveness of their enterprises. In this situation the British Labour Party, and the British left generally, was handicapped by its continued 'Keynesian' approach to economic policy. It saw its role as maintaining full employment and *distributing* income and wealth more 'fairly' or 'justly', but not as 'interfering' with wealth *creation*. (That, it seemed, could be left entirely to British capitalists and 'their' Conservative Party.) In short, I argued that the British Left had a politics which made sense in the context of a dynamic and successful capitalism (and which tended to do best, electorally, in times of relative prosperity) but which was inadequate to deal with the difficult policy problems posed by an ever more struggling British capitalism.

This analysis did not, however, lead me to endorse neo-liberal (or what were then called 'monetarist') economic policies. Although I had reservations about the performance of some nationalised industries, I never supported the privatisation of natural monopolies such as railways or energy and water utilities. Nor did I think that the competitiveness of British industry could be restored simply by lowering its tax 'burden' or enacting 'labour market reforms' to weaken trade unions and strengthen the power of employers. In my view, shared by a number of other economists, the fundamental problem of British industry, and of the British economy generally, was a failure to technologically innovate and modernise and to invest on the scale and in the manner required to maintain national and international competitiveness. I was therefore, and still am, a strong believer in a state-directed 'industry policy', on a broadly Japanese or Korean model, designed to encourage and assist existing UK-based industries to modernise, to maintain or increase market share and to facilitate new 'start-ups' in sectors with rapid growth potential.

However, I was remiss in not making this policy preference clearer in the book (although it is strongly implied in its last chapter) and in thus allowing space for reading it in 'Blairite' ways. Despite this however, I believe that this central theme of *Rethinking Socialism*, - the severe shortcomings of gradualist social democracy when confronted with a failing or misfiring capitalism – remains as pertinent now as it was in 1983. Then, as now, far too much self-identified 'radical' or 'left-wing' thought in Britain consists of decontextualized, economically naïve moralising.

But if it is still pertinent in this way, other aspects of the book have been severely outdated by changes over the last 36 years. Firstly, the period from the early 1980s to the present has seen the rapid and deep *globalisation* of the world economy. This has had a mass of effects which cannot be dealt with here, (although I have written about them elsewhere). One of the most significant of them has been the narrowing of the space for national economic policy-making of any type, and most especially for policies which are uncongenial to global financial and capital markets. In fact, if 'social democratic' policies are to be carried out effectively now, they *have* to be pursued at the trans-national as well as the national level. For if they are not, they can easily be undermined or nullified by currency attacks and/or capital flight. In short, its lack of any analysis of capitalism as a global system is one respect in which *Rethinking Socialism* is seriously out-dated.

The other is its treatment of feminism, which is almost entirely concerned with socialist feminism. But socialist feminism has been marginalised to the point of irrelevance in the development of second wave feminism since the 1980s. Feminism *is* now 'liberal feminism' in its organising assumptions and policy concerns, and *Rethinking Socialism* seriously underestimated its political potential in that form. In fact, liberal feminism (concerned exclusively with increasing gender equality throughout civil society) has been, along with neo-liberalism, the most influential political ideology of the late twentieth and early twenty-first centuries. And now it is producing deep social, cultural and political reverberations in virtually every human society on the planet. And whilst I continue to have some reservations about its exclusive focus on gender equality (whatever happened to class, for example?) it would be churlish not to recognise, and applaud, the empowerment and hope liberal feminism has provided, and is providing, for half the world's population. If only one could say anything remotely similar about socialism!

GNK
Sydney,
23rd January 2019

Rethinking Socialism

A THEORY FOR A BETTER PRACTICE

Gavin Kitching

METHUEN
LONDON AND NEW YORK

First published in 1983 by
Methuen & Co. Ltd
11 New Fetter Lane,
London EC4P 4EE
Published in the USA by
Methuen & Co.
in association with Methuen, Inc.
733 Third Avenue,
New York, NY 10017

© 1983 Gavin Kitching

Printed in Great Britain by
Richard Clay (The Chaucer Press) Ltd
Bungay, Suffolk

British Library Cataloguing in
Publication Data

Kitching, Gavin
Rethinking socialism.
1. Socialism
I. Title
335   HX73
ISBN 0-416-35840-3

Library of Congress Cataloging
in Publication Data

Kitching, G. N.
Rethinking socialism.

1. Socialism—Great Britain.
2. Socialism. I. Title.
HX244.K56 1983 335'.1 83-12104
ISBN 0-416-35840-3 (pbk.)

Everything that can be thought at all can be thought clearly.
Everything that can be put into words can be put clearly.
Wittgenstein, *Tractatus Logico-Philosophicus*

For Angela

Contents

Foreword

The General Election occurred as this book was going to press. Late in time, but early enough that I might, had I wished, have altered certain sections of the manuscript (particularly perhaps the beginning of the final chapter) to take account of this further débâcle for the Left. I have decided not to do so. I think it better that the book remain in its original form, partly because in the immediate aftermath of such a disaster it is easy, in depression and frustration, to go 'over the top' in one's own judgements and generalizations. Saturday, June 11th 1983 is still too soon for the dust to have settled and for an in-depth analysis of the results to have been undertaken.

More importantly, however, I have chosen to leave the book as it is because I hope that its political force may be greater if it is unambiguously clear that it was finished three months before the General Election was even announced, and indeed that the first draft was completed by February 1982. Not that I would wish to claim much credit for whatever predictive accuracy it may possess. That the next General Election would result in a Tory victory was obvious to anybody with what my father would have termed 'an ounce of political nouse'. I also think that the extent of that victory was actually greater than can be accounted for by the factors discussed in this book. Quite apart from the 'Falklands factor', it must also be said that the Labour Party fought an electoral campaign which it would be flattering to call inept. But it did so because its leadership and its membership remain fundamentally divided, and on one side of that divide – and currently predominant – is the Left of the Labour Party whose weak-minded utopianism is analysed in these pages. Thus I do think that the kind of Left politics that I discuss in this book, and more importantly the fundamental long-term social changes that have both produced a constituency base for such a politics and rendered its chances of electoral success effectively nil, are at the root of the awful situation facing the Labour Party. Until the party develops a politics that truly faces up to the complexities of a Britain basically transformed by 25 years of sustained capitalist boom, it will, in my view, be doomed to continued decline and marginalization. And yet those changes could be harnessed to the support of a new type of socialist politics. I outline in this book some elements which I think such a politics will have to contain. Much is missing, much needs to be clarified, qualified and developed, but I submit that it at least represents a start.

There is more I could add, but I will not. Instead I will express just one hope. I hope that the Left in the Labour Party will not respond to this perfectly foreseeable and avoidable electoral disaster with any more nonsense about the nasty media, or how the Left case was somehow 'not got across'. For if one thing is obvious, even 48 hours after the election, it is that had the message been 'got across' – plainly, fairly and in all its implications – the defeat would have been even greater. I had the somewhat rare experience of canvassing in a southern constituency which Labour managed to win, and it was very clear that even those who did vote Labour did so despite, rather than because of, the policies in its manifesto. It is quite likely that their loyalty will not stand even one further test if those policies are not changed.

I said I hoped for a new realism on the Left. Judging from remarks attributed to Mr Livingstone and Mr Mullin in today's papers, that hope is to be disappointed. Truly there is none so blind as he who will not see.

Preface

This book was written in anger. I have become convinced that most left-wing people in this country (counting as left-wing all those people from the Bennite wing of the Labour Party leftwards) are wasting their time. They are wasting their time, politically, because a large part of their views and assumptions about the world are totally at odds with those of the bulk of the people whom they are trying to persuade. They are also wasting their time because those views and beliefs, and the 'ghetto' situation in which most socialists in this country live, lead them to behave in ways which by alienating even potentially sympathetic people are self-defeating. The net result of all this is that 'socialism' as a concept and as a possible and desirable alternative to the kind of society in which we now live is fast losing all credibility. Already, in the wake of the SDP there is a determined attempt to replace socialism by 'social democracy' as the only legitimate form of Left politics in Britain. Soon, socialism, like communism, may be relegated to the status of a political dirty word.

In this situation I want to do two things. I want firstly to
explain as clearly as possible to socialists in Britain why I think
they are wasting their time. Secondly, I want to suggest not only
to them but also to a much wider audience what I think a more
practically viable socialist strategy for Britain might be. However, these two tasks do not fit easily together in one short book.
The first requires me to deal with some issues in economic and
political theory which will be familiar to most people acquainted
with socialist ideas and the history of socialist thought, but which
may not be so readily comprehensible to others. The second
requires that to try and reach as wide an audience as possible, I
must keep exotic vocabulary and socialist 'in-group' references to
a minimum. Moreover, since I hope the second part of my
argument (the suggestions for an alternative) follows logically
from the first (an analysis of the shortcomings in current socialist
theory and practice), then the whole thing, including the
theoretical critique, must be comprehensible to as wide an
audience as possible.

Given these aims, and because I do not conceive this book as
addressed primarily to Left intellectuals, I have opted for what I
hope is a clear, plain and unjargonized prose, even when I have
felt that some subtlety of meaning or nuance has been lost in
doing so. Secondly, I have opted to dispense entirely with the
academic references which books like this are usually full of.
Where I am directly indebted to another person's work for a
quotation or for a table of statistics I have included a reference,
but elsewhere I have risked making assertions and constructing
arguments without footnotes to cover my back. This is partly
because this book owes as much to personal experience as to
academic reading, but also because I think that the intellectual
Left's current style of writing and speaking is part of its problem,
not part of the solution. Therefore, though what appears below
owes much to the influence of Antonio Gramsci, the later work
of Nicos Poulantzas, Trevor Pateman, Sheila Rowbotham,
Barrington Moore, Gwyn Williams, Isaac Deutscher, Edward
Thompson, Leszak Kolakowski, Bill Warren, and, as they say,

'many, many more', this is the first and in many cases the only time their names will appear in this book.

I have, however, made one compromise in this cult of plainness and in avoiding the theoretically difficult or exotic. In Chapter 3 I briefly review some ideas from Edward Thompson's book *The Poverty of Theory* as a prelude to a discussion and criticism of what I call the 'romantic anti-capitalism' prevalent in socialist circles in Britain, especially on the Left of the Labour Party. In the course of the chapter a number of rather more abstruse theoretical and philosophical issues (concerning Marx's understanding of society and history) are referred to. They are not discussed in depth since they are not strictly necessary to the essentially political purposes of the chapter. However, any reader who *is* interested in following this debate further can do so in the appendix to this book, a lengthy essay on politics, economics and intellectuals. However, it is an appendix precisely because it is an optional extra. It is by no means essential to following the central argument of the book.

I also have some debts to acknowledge. 'Romantic', or as he would call it 'radical', anti-capitalism is a concept which I acquired from Michael Cowen, though I cannot say whether he would approve of the use to which it is put here. To Anthea Thomas I owe long overdue thanks for typing yet another manuscript so promptly and well, and to Nancy Marten I am deeply indebted for efforts, far beyond the call of duty, as my editor. Finally, my thanks to Bernard Crick for his warm support and propaganda efforts on my behalf and to David Rosenberg for shoring up the confidence of a writer venturing outside his allotted academic 'field' for the first time.

Introduction

This book aims to reinstate an evolutionary and gradualist
perspective at the centre of socialist politics and thought about
socialism. My central thesis is that the construction of socialist
societies and a socialist world will take a very long time (probably
centuries) and that an essential prerequisite of such a world
coming into being is a high degree of material prosperity and a
citizenry of considerable skill, knowledge and intellectual sophistication. I also argue that because the development of capitalist
societies (societies in which the means of production and
distribution are private property owned and controlled by a small
minority) both creates a generalized (though highly unequal)
material prosperity and leads to the emergence and expansion of
an ever more sophisticated working class, it provides conditions
which may be conducive to socialist construction in the long
term. However, the development of such conditions is uneven
and only part of a highly contradictory process. There is nothing
inevitable about the emergence of socialism from advanced
capitalism and the matter will be determined by social and

political struggle (conscious human activity) whose outcome is always (in the present and future) an open question. The word 'struggle' here is not used metaphorically. I have in mind continuous social conflict which may at times be violent, especially when crucial issues of power are being decided. However, such dramatic moments may alternate with long periods when conflict is much more muted and constitutional, though none the less real for that. Thus my gradualist and evolutionary perspective is not a simple advocacy of incremental social reform, though there may be periods of such reform. It is rather the rejection of any 'cataclysmic' notion of the process of socialist revolution, such that the coming of socialism out of advanced capitalism will be datable to some hour, day or year. In fact, I think it quite likely that if Britain or any other advanced capitalist country reaches a state which many radicals in the 1980s would regard as 'the achievement of socialism', debate and struggle will long ago have shifted to other terrain with other concepts and 'socialism v. capitalism' will no longer be the issue. An impatient world, then as now, may leave it to historians looking back to announce that some process of 'revolutionary' change has been completed since those far off days of the late twentieth century.

Thus I reject a cataclysmic, 'barricades' conception of socialist revolution against advanced capitalism and adopt a gradualist and evolutionary (but not reformist) concept of socialist construction. I also believe that a necessary but not sufficient condition of the creation of socialism is a materially prosperous society. And I believe that socialism is impossible to construct in materially poor and deprived societies. Or rather, I believe that 'socialism in backward and underdeveloped countries has a powerful tendency to become a backward and underdeveloped socialism'.*

Such a position need not and does not involve a lack of

---

*Paul Baran, *The Political Economy of Growth*, New York, Monthly Review Press, 1957, p. 9.

understanding of and sympathy for socialist regimes in poor countries, and certainly there is little point in a dogmatic denial of the right of these societies to call themselves socialist. In so far as they have abolished private property in the means of production, distribution and exchange they *are* socialist. They are *not*, however, *socialist democracies*, and since I hold that recognizably democratic political and constitutional forms are an integral part of socialism, then I regard the socialism of these states as a poor and stunted thing, a 'backward and under-developed socialism' in Baran's phrase.

I hold that these societies are not socialist democracies because (a) many of them are poor and poverty has certain social and cultural consequences which mean that there is little or no effective popular support for democratic forms, and (b) they build socialist economic institutions primarily in order to commence or speed up the process of industrialization and economic growth. Such a process is, I believe, incompatible with meaningful democracy, because it is so unpleasant for the majority of the population in the societies affected by it that if such people had any genuine control over political and economic power they would use it to prevent such a process occurring. Since certain élites in these countries have an interest in this process succeeding and believe that its success is in the interests of the long-term welfare of their people, they will not allow this popular will open or effective expression.

Thus, I am committed to a two-sided conception that (1) socialist *democracy* is incompatible with poverty and primitive accumulation, and (2) such democracy is more compatible with, and feasible in, materially prosperous societies. To repeat, however: to assert (2) is not to assert that socialist democracy *will* emerge in materially prosperous societies, only that the opportunities for such emergence are greater than in poor societies.

This conception also implies that as socialist dictatorships succeed in becoming more materially prosperous, the possibility of their conversion into genuinely democratic socialist societies increases. I think that recent events in Poland and eastern Europe show this to be true. However, once again I must stress that there is nothing inevitable about this process. The conversion of a socialist dictatorship into a socialist democracy must be struggled for and that struggle may be long and bitter. However, because industrialization and economic growth under socialist dictatorships create material demands and expectations which they cannot meet and (more importantly) create a sophisticated and informed working class able and willing to assert its own power, socialist dictatorships may be seen, historically, as generating the conditions for their own demise.

However, in this book I do not deal, other than peripherally, with the struggle for democratic rights in Russia and eastern Europe or with problems of socialist construction in the Third World. Rather, I am concerned with the second part of my two-sided conception: that advanced capitalist societies provide opportunities for the construction of socialist democracy. I concentrate on this because it is directly relevant to the current political situation in Britain and because most socialists today believe the contrary. They believe it is obvious that with every capitalist boom in the west these societies have moved *further and further away* from socialism and are irredeemably lost in a de-politicizing materialism and reformism. I will argue against this position in all the chapters which follow, and will suggest that the situation is more hopeful than this. It may become even more hopeful, I argue, if capitalism can overcome its current crisis and re-establish long boom conditions again. I also suggest a strategy for use by the Left in Britain which may help to alleviate the capitalist crisis here *and* generate substantial gains for the working class.

However, to see the real opportunities for socialist advance brought by the further development of capitalism in the west, it is necessary to have a rather different conception of socialism, particularly of socialist democracy, than that to which most socialists in Britain are currently committed and to have a rather different conception of the working class, especially of its 'vanguard', than that which is generally held. I argue in fact for radical changes in socialist theory and practice in order to seize the opportunities that exist for socialist construction in Britain and elsewhere in the west. The first chapter sets out what those changes should be in very general terms and defends them with reference to a conception of socialism which I believe would have found favour with Marx, though it is continually negated in theory and practice by many contemporary Marxists. The second, third and fourth chapters deepen this general critique with reference to (1) the problems of socialism in poor countries and their implications for socialism in general; (2) romantic anti-capitalism which I believe is very powerful on the Left in Britain; and (3) the theory and practice of socialist feminism. The fifth and final chapter derives from the principles set out in the previous four a transitional programme for socialism in Britain in response to the current economic crisis.

One further introductory remark is in order. Running all through this book is a belief that for socialists, and indeed for human beings in general, hope for a better and more democratic future is no mere 'optimism of the will' battling valiantly with a 'pessimism of the intellect' to which it should, rationally, demur. I am struck again and again in much contemporary thought, self-advertised as 'Marxist', how Marx's name is continually invoked in support of a cataclysmic revolutionism, whose justification is to save the world from the doom to which it is otherwise destined, ecologically, demographically, or through nuclear holocaust.*

* A note is necessary here in order to avoid misunderstanding. These remarks should not be taken to mean that I think these dangers to our species to be imaginary. On the contrary, I am a member of CND because I take the last danger very seriously indeed, and in fact as a lot more likely to produce the end of the human race – at least at the moment – than either ecological problems or population growth. The point, however, is that I do not think that the coming of national 'socialisms' will, in themselves, diminish the danger of nuclear war (and may, in fact, depending upon the precise circumstances of their creation, increase it). And if we have to wait for *international* socialism before nuclear disarmament or effective measures to check pollution of the seas (for example) can be contemplated, then the prospects for the human race look gloomy indeed. It is because I believe that the arguments for unilateral nuclear disarmament both can and must be separated from any and all arguments for socialism that I support CND being what it is, a broadly-based popular campaign drawing on people who are not, and do not wish to be, socialists in any form.

But Marx was, in the end, a Victorian. For very good reasons stemming from the industrial transformation of Europe which he witnessed in his own lifetime, he believed in both the possibility and the actuality of progress in human society. Indeed, his primary objection to capitalism was that whilst potentially it held out for the first time the prospect of a genuinely human life for the majority of mankind, its structure and internal dynamics meant that that potential was constantly frustrated. The whole aim of the socialist transformation of capitalism was thus to turn potentiality into actuality. Where Marx and Engels diverged from so many of their contemporaries was *not* therefore in a rejection of the concept of progress in history but in their understanding of the nature of that progress. For them, progress was a highly discontinuous and contradictory process in which, in all class societies, the very processes building 'the productive forces' were at the same time processes of class exploitation and oppression. Engels' famous remark about progress – 'History is the cruellest of all Goddesses. She drives her chariot through heaps of the slain' – has been seen as the apogee of 'historical determinism' and drove Karl Popper* apopleptic. But it was not a prospective defence of Stalin's labour camps or even a 'meta-historical' judgement held to be true eternally for all times and places. It was simply colourful presentation of what Engels took to be a broad empirical generalization about the course of European history up to and including the nineteenth century. The whole aim of socialist transformation for Marx and Engels was to *end* that historical situation by substituting for the exploitative and bloody progress of class society a consciously controlled and planned progress in which 'the free development of each' was to be the condition of 'the free development of all'. A lot easier said than done as we have subsequently learnt, and as all of what follows will stress. But for Marx and Engels it was both possible and necessary because the very development of capitalism would

* Karl Popper, *The Open Society and its Enemies*, vol. 2, London, Routledge & Kegan Paul, 1952.

both reveal the necessity for such a transformation and, to a degree, provide the means and conditions for its accomplishment. This being said, however, human beings and particularly the working class (which for Marx and Engels meant the vast majority of human beings living under capitalism) still had to use those means and conditions to actively *make* that transformation. There could be no guarantee that it would happen, but Marx and Engels were cautiously optimistic that it would, primarily because each further development of capitalism revealed its essential irrationality more and more clearly, and they believed that rational human beings could not coexist indefinitely with irrational social systems. This belief was essentially a matter of faith, resting as it does ultimately on a view of human beings as essentially rational creatures (indeed distinguished from other creatures primarily by their rationality). It is a faith which I share, and sharing it I share the cautious optimism which it generates.

Their optimism was cautious, however, because Marx and Engels also believed that the bearers of this rationality were real human beings living and acting in particular societies at particular times. It was, therefore, axiomatic for them that this rationality could be, and most frequently was, put to sectional uses, to the pursuit of particular material and ideal goals that frequently involved the exploitation, neglect and repression of other human beings. The exploited, consequently, were forced to use their rationality both as a means of survival and as a means of resistance. Moreover, for any particular group of human beings, rational activity always occurred in a 'given' (inherited from previous generations) set of material and institutional conditions, and was bounded by those conditions whilst at the same time reinforcing them and from time to time changing them. Thus it was that actions of a minority (a ruling class) which might at one historical period be exploitative of the majority, or at least of large sections of the population, might yet issue in material results from which subsequent generations (including the descendants of the previously exploited) could benefit. Thus for Marx and Engels, progress in and through all class societies had been real and bloody, not the less real because bloody, but not the less bloody because real. For them, the essence of historical understanding lay in fully recognizing and not shrinking from either side of that dialectic, and retaining one's optimism, not despite it but because of it. For me, this clear-eyed, unromantic, but unremitting humanism remains an inspiring example and a source in itself both of knowledge about the present and of hope for the future. This book is my attempt to write in that spirit.

A note on class

Discussions of socialism, particularly in Britain, are continually bedevilled by two very different concepts of the working class. In Marx himself, and in much Marxist discussion, the concept refers to *all* those people who live by selling their labour power and who have in fact no other means of survival since they do not own or control 'means of production' (land, buildings, machinery, stocks and shares). THIS IS THE MAIN USAGE WHICH I ADOPT THROUGHOUT THIS BOOK. In Britain, in the 1980s of course, this means that the working class comprises men, women, blacks, browns and whites, doctors and dockers, sales executives and sales assistants, university teachers and bus inspectors. Given this definition, the working class so defined comprises the vast majority of people in this country now, as it did when Marx wrote. However, although much Left discussion and political activism *starts* with this concept and distinguishes it sharply from more conventional sociological and popular uses of the term 'working class' (to refer, for example, to skilled and unskilled manual workers), I argue in all of what follows that THE MAJOR IMPLICATIONS OF ADOPTING THIS 'CLASSICAL' CONCEPT IN WESTERN CAPITALIST SOCIETIES TODAY ARE NEVER REALLY FOL-LOWED THROUGH EITHER IN LEFT THEORY, OR INDEED IN LEFT PRACTICE. The major implication, as I see it, is that the bulk of the Left's political constituency, so defined, are people who (to borrow a phrase from American politics) 'are neither black, poor, nor radical'. In fact, no sooner has one set up the classical concept and applied it to the current situation than one runs up against this uncomfortable fact. Thus, in practice, Left political usage of the term tends constantly to slip back to the more orthodox sociological use. That is, socialists today may *begin* by paying formal homage to Marx's concept of the working class, but they very soon revert in theory and, more importantly, in practice, to concentration upon the manual working class. Once this has happened, of course, it then becomes possible and necessary to distinguish the 'working class' from the 'middle class' with the latter being distinguished in a variety of ways (from white-collar status to speech patterns), depending upon the context of this discussion. In other words, Marxists and socialists in Britain tend to use *both* a Marxist class vocabulary (working class/ bourgeoisie) *and* what may be termed a 'popular' British class vocabulary (working class/middle class/upper middle class), depending upon whom they are speaking to and what they are speaking about. Since I live in Britain now, I am as much heir to this ambiguous vocabulary as anyone else, and to the possibilities of confusion which it brings. However, since I want what follows to be comprehensible and easy to follow I do not feel it wise to adopt a strained or forced vocabulary of exotic terms to keep the distinction clear. I have therefore opted for a procedure which I hope buys clarity at the cost of a certain cumbersomness.

When I use the term working class *without* quotation marks it is to be taken to refer to *all* those people in Britain who live by selling their labour power. When I use the terms 'working class' and 'middle class' in quotation marks I am either reporting on someone else's use of the more orthodox sociological concepts or adopting those concepts myself for some specific purpose. There are, of course, an enormous number of theoretical and political problems which follow from the insistence that we should continue to base both socialist theory and socialist politics upon the retention of the classical concept, problems which all stem, in one way or another, from the changes which have occurred in capitalist societies since Marx wrote. I deal with some (though not all) of those problems in the chapters that follow.

So, in short,

the working class	=	all those people who live by selling their labour power for a wage or salary
the 'working class'	=	skilled and unskilled manual workers.

1 / Socialism and the working class

Introduction

Any work with such an ambitious title as *Rethinking Socialism* stands in serious danger of pretentiousness. A series of essentially speculative ideas such as the ones which follow are perhaps just acceptable from the pen of an ageing scholar looking back on a lifetime's work and seeking its summation and meaning. Coming in fact from someone in his mid-thirties whose corpus of empirical work and political and human experience is still quite limited, it positively invites suspicion.

My defence is twofold. In the first place, the issues discussed in this book have concerned me for the best part of the last ten years and have been a part of my political experience since I became active on the Left as a teenager. Secondly, I feel that the current situation in Britain and in the western world in general requires socialists to look at their historical theory and practice with particular honesty, with a painful honesty if necessary, for never in the post-war period has there been such a gap between apparent opportunity and minimal achievement. Capitalism currently faces the deepest crisis, both nationally and internationally, that it has known since the 1930s, and yet the political influence of the Marxist Left, certainly in the advanced capitalist countries, remains miniscule. This contrast, this powerlessness and irrelevance amidst what should 'theoretically' be a period of growing influence and power has led to a widespread gloom and demoralization on the Left. Responses to it have varied. Some socialists, in Britain particularly, have thrown in their lot with the Bennite Left of the Labour Party; others have entered single-issue campaigns (of which the revived national and international campaigns for nuclear disarmament are currently the most popular). And others have withdrawn from politics totally.

In my view, such gloom and despondency is unjustified and springs from an inadequate understanding of the relationship between capitalist crisis and socialist advance. I will argue that contrary to what is still the dominant view on the communist and Trotskyist Left and indeed even among Left social democrats, advances toward socialism are much more likely to occur in capitalist booms. The whole post-war history of the western world shows this clearly. However, to see this requires a basic shift in our understanding of what socialism is and of the role of the 'working class' in socialist construction. I shall argue that such a shift is totally compatible with the spirit of Marx's understanding of socialism, though it certainly is *not* compatible with what is popularly presented as the dominant Marxist view of the transition to socialism in advanced capitalist economies (which still depends, in one way or another, on a 'breakdown' thesis). The shift I have in mind does not involve denying the dominant role of the working class in socialist construction, but it does involve rethinking who the working class is. Above all it requires a much more historically flexible conception of which people constitute the most economically central and politically advanced sections of that class.

The working class

The 'note on class' at the end of the introduction announced my intention to use the term *working class* to refer to all those people in Britain who earn their living by selling their 'labour power' (i.e. their physical and mental abilities) for a wage or salary. Classically, these people are to be distinguished both from 'the bourgeoisie' who own and control the means of production under capitalism (land, buildings, machinery, raw materials, stocks and shares) and the 'petty bourgeoisie' (owners of small quantities of capital such as small shopkeepers and workshop owners). The future prospects for democratic socialism in Britain depend entirely upon how far it can recruit the working class, as classically defined above, to public and political activity which is either explicitly or implicitly socialist in its import. The notion of 'implicit socialism' in particular depends upon a particular understanding of socialism which is presented in the second part of this chapter. Here, I want to deal with a number of problems which arise from maintaining the classical concept of the working class as the constituency for socialism in the Britain of the 1980s.

The first, and certainly the most important and difficult of these problems is the enormous occupational and status differentiation of the working class which has taken place in capitalism since the mid-nineteenth century. Marx was living and writing at a time when the bulk of the people who were working class, in the sense of being sellers of labour power, were also 'working class' in the sense of being manual workers. This fact, together with the general similarity of social conditions and ways of life of many manual workers, meant that it was comparatively easy for Marx to conceive the possibility, indeed the likelihood, that the labour-power-selling working class would also become 'class conscious', that is, would share a sense of a common situation and a common enemy and would come to act both socially and politically upon that sense of shared identity and interests. There is much debate about how far that actually happened in Britain or elsewhere. But leaving aside this historical question it seems obvious that in contemporary Britain no such sense of common class identity or interest exists among the working class. On the contrary, many working-class people think of themselves as 'middle class' for a variety of reasons, ranging from the non-manual nature of their work to the places and types of houses in which they live and the way they speak. They certainly feel no sense of common identity with the manual 'working class'. Socialists in fact find themselves echoing the apoplectic doctor or solicitor ('What's all this nonsense about "workers" and "the working class", I'm working class, aren't I, I work, don't I?!'), with the difference that socialists take the point with a certain theoretical seriousness, whereas the 'we're all working class' school of invective is engaged in what is seen as polemical destruction by absurdity.

However, I believe that the way socialists should confront this central problem with their notion of the working class is not by quietly sliding back to the manual 'working class' (which means, now, to a minority of the adult British population), but by attempting to use the *one* common identity which all these people do share – their identity as *citizens* of a parliamentary democracy. Their aim in fact should be to encourage any and all activities which involve *turning a passive citizenry into an active one* (even if they are active in ways – see below – which are mutually contradictory). They should do this not because the creation of such a citizenry will itself construct socialism, but because without it the construction of *democratic* socialism is impossible. However, the creation of such a citizenry will also, I think, be helpful to the cause of socialism and certainly it will be of more aid to socialists than their opponents. The reasons for my believing this are set out later in this chapter and are indeed a central theme of this book.

The second major difficulty with maintaining the classical concept of the working class in contemporary Britain derives from certain aspects of Marxist theory – particularly ideas concerned with 'productive' and 'unproductive' labour under capitalism and the related question of the economic centrality of certain workers to capitalism. In a book which is primarily concerned with practical politics, I do not wish to explore the theoretical issues involved in Marx's value theory or in his theory of 'productive' workers – those who are the source of 'surplus value' (and thus of profit) for capitalism. Suffice to say that I do

not think Marx's distinction between productive and unproductive labour can be sustained, and that, especially when questions
of the 'realization' of surplus value (rather than its simple
production) are raised, *no* workers can be regarded as 'unproductive' for capitalism. It is true, however, and one does not
need to be a Marxist to recognize this, that some workers earn
their wages as a share of output whilst others earn them from
'revenue', i.e. from money derived from that output in the form of
taxes or rates.

The argument that some workers should be central to Left
activity because they have noticeably more bargaining power
than others (miners, dockers, transport workers, certain groups
of engineers) is rather more serious politically. For it is much
more frequently encountered in political debate on the Left (the
more abstruse issues above about 'productive labour' and
'surplus value' being generally consigned to the weekend school
or seminar room). A more inclusive notion of the working class, it
is argued, overlooks this question of the greater economic
strength of some parts of that class, as well as the traditions of
organization and 'militancy' of some of these more powerful
workers (miners, dockers, etc.). However, I believe that this view
is based on a fundamentally mistaken equation between economic militancy and strength (most often used in a purely
defensive fashion) and socialist potential. This equation or
conflation is in turn generated by a particular view of the most
potent causes of revolution and social transformation. This view,
which I call a 'breakdown' or 'big bang' theory of revolution, sees
the greatest potential for socialist transformation in periods of
economic crisis, and in particular in the material want and
suffering which some groups of workers experience in such crises.
This idea (which certainly has great warrant in Marx's own
writing) then tends to lead to a strategy of supporting *any* group
of workers who are waging defensive struggles against capitalism
to preserve or enhance their standard of living. In particular, the
struggles of workers to resist closures and redundancies brought
about by economic crises and by the less spectacular long-term

processes of change in a capitalist economy have been viewed very positively in a great deal of socialist history (see Chapter 3) and tend to receive automatic support in contemporary socialist practice. Such 'defensive' struggles may well be extremely 'militant' in the sense of involving strikes, occupations and political campaigning, but far from marking advances toward socialism they are perfectly compatible with, and indeed partly the product of, a form of profoundly anti-socialist class consciousness.

The third major difficulty with the adoption of the classical concept of the working class in the contemporary capitalist situation is that such an enormously differentiated and diverse class as this, it is argued, cannot possibly engage in any kind of united '*collective*' action against capitalism. No material basis exists for such collective unity. One is talking, it is said, about millions of people who have such enormously varied occupations, life styles, incomes, work and living conditions that they cannot possibly form any kind of common consciousness, let alone coalesce around any common political strategy or programme.

I think there is a strong sense in which this is true, and a weak sense in which it is false. If by 'collective action' one means some united, collective action of the *whole* class – 'one big union' or something similar – then this objection holds. If, however, one means that members of the working class so conceived never combine together in groups or organizations to achieve political or social goals, then this view is false. Millions of members of the working class in Britain are unionized, but even if one leaves aside unions (which is what Left people usually mean in fact by 'collective action'), then we see workers involved in consumer groups, tenants' associations, residents' association, ecology pressure groups, football supporters' clubs, ratepayers' associations, anti-vivisectionist campaigns, and so. This public activity by people within the working class is to be encouraged, for in so far as public activity extends and deepens – and with it the scope both of politics and public life generally – the chances for a transition to socialism increase.

There is one final and important point which should be made in this initial defence of my very broad concept of the working class. It could simply be objected that in insisting upon the need to maintain the classical concept, all I am doing is opting for a populist politics in place of a class politics. Am I not simply positing some kind of 'popular' cross-class coalition in which 'the people' are mobilized against a lowest common denominator enemy (like 'monopoly capital') in a manner already suggested both by Left social democrats and 'Eurocommunists'? No, this book is not an argument for such a populist strategy because it does not conceive that the working-class-as-citizenry is recruitable in current conditions to any single political programme or objective, not even a minimalist 'anti-monopoly' one. On the contrary, much of the collective and/or public activity to which different groups of workers are recruitable is mutually contradictory. It involves 'middle-class' workers opposing 'working-class' workers, men opposing women, black workers opposing white workers, in activities which are oppositional because they reflect real differences of interest. The point is that the generalization of a conflictual public life of this sort would itself be a powerful move towards transcending the minority public life and the mass passivity upon which parliamentary democracy depends as a political system, and upon which capitalism depends as an economic system.

This involves abandoning a profound ambiguity in the Left towards such mass involvement in public life, an ambiguity which is rarely expressed publicly but which is a powerful determinant of much actual Left political activity. For, of course, if one's politics are based upon views which one knows not to be widely shared, one will necessarily view the extension and deepening of public life somewhat ambiguously. Thus, it is awful that ordinary union members are not more involved in union business, but one is relieved that the attendance at the branch is so low tonight because we might be able to get this resolution on Chile through! Thus, one wishes to bring 'the pressure of public opinion' to bear upon the Home Office about the conditions in our prisons, but the 'public opinion' involved can't be too 'public'

because one knows full well what the polls tell us about the way
the majority of people want to see offenders treated. Of course
parliamentary democracy is a sham democracy dominated by the
bourgeoisie, but thank God it's MPs and not the masses who vote
on capital punishment!

This uncomfortable ambiguity, verging at times on dishonesty,
exists not because of some 'false consciousness' on the Left,
but because of the realities of politics in our present society.
These realities are based upon the passivity and ignorance
of a considerable majority of our citizenry and the activity
and knowledge of a minority (of which the Left is part – but only
a part). Further:

(1) Passivity and ignorance are not coincidentally but causally
related: the politically ignorant are ignorant because they are
passive and passive because they are ignorant. A way therefore
has to be found to break this mutually reinforcing syndrome.

(2) Increased material prosperity (and especially capitalist
booms) tend to expand the active citizenry and thus reduce the
size of the passive majority. They do this by releasing workers
from a concern with purely private and material forms of self-
fulfilment and allowing them to become more active citizens,
seeking other kinds of self-fulfilment in the public domain. This
does not mean necessarily that they will become 'progressive' or
'left-wing' active citizens. They may join the National Front or
(more likely and more commonly) join a local or national
campaign to reduce taxes and rates and the 'wasteful' public
services which are dependent upon them. However, seen from the
perspective offered in this book, this is still an historical advance.
For any breach in passivity is a permanent breach (in the sense
that it is likely to be passed on in families, in teaching children
'the importance of politics'). Moreover, looked at in long-term
historical perspective, the Left will never see any substantial
advances towards socialism so long as it operates a politics
depending in reality (if not in theory or rhetoric) upon mass
passivity. The reason for this is, of course, that as long as it is so
dependent its bluff can be called. Right-wing Labour leaders can

appeal over the heads of constituency party organizations to even more right-wing Labour voters; the NCB can conscript a majority of miners against Arthur Scargill; *The Sun* newspaper can call down popular prejudices upon feminists, homosexuals, striking workers, and so on. In short, unlike the Right, the Left cannot do without an active, informed majority of citizens, because without such a majority of citizen-workers it cannot win. 'Democratic élitism' – democracy as a public life of competing minorities – holds out no hope for the Left, even in the long term. Our first task therefore is to transcend it, and that in itself, if I am right, is going to take considerable time.

This mention of time takes us to the next issue. For up to this point I have dealt with the issue of class in purely 'comparative static' terms, i.e. by considering the situation now and the situation when Marx wrote and noting the changes which have occurred in the working class in the intervening period. But I have given no attention to the actual processes by which such changes have been, and are, produced. This involves an exploration of the relationship between the working class and capitalism as an economic system, and in particular with the changes in capitalism of which changes in the working class are a part.

The working class and capitalist development

The working class as a part of a constantly changing capitalism is itself a changing entity, whose occupational and sexual composition, educational level, and social and cultural outlook are continually shifting in very complex and uneven ways. It is a pronounced weakness of the traditional Left that in this changing situation it continues to concentrate its efforts on sections of the working class that are politically regressive and indeed that are in decline economically. This is because, as I have already said, the Left constantly mistakes the defensive struggles of marginalized workers (struggles which may, in a traditional sense, by extremely 'militant') for revolutionary or proto-revolutionary struggle.

This tendency of the Left to concentrate its efforts on the manual 'working class' and to throw its efforts into every defensive struggle waged by sections of that class which are in decline coexists with a total lack of class awareness amongst the Left intelligentsia itself. Thus for many Left intellectuals (taking this term in its broadest sense to embrace far more than professional academics or teachers) the question is always posed as the need for 'us' (the Left intelligentsia and activists *conceived as individuals*) to reach and convert 'them' ('the working class'). However, even a cursory examination of the class composition of most constituency Labour parties, and indeed of most Left gatherings in general, indicates that activists are themselves part of a certain quite discernible section of the working class. Very broadly this section is made up of white-collar workers mainly in the public sector, but with a minority private sector group as well. The occupational categories involved are familiar enough: local and central government civil servants, teachers, artists, musicians, social and community workers, journalists. There is also a scattering of more technically orientated white-collar workers, including technicians, architects and engineers. The Left is particularly strong among all those workers of these latter categories who are active in the trade union movement. Indeed this is often one major characteristic differentiating socialists from non-socialists, particularly among more technical workers.

Thus I would argue that the Left in Britain and in western Europe generally, does have quite a strong base within the working class, but not within those sections of that class about which it is typically obsessed. There is every reason to believe that with the further development of capitalism most of the categories identified will grow (particularly public and private sector service workers), whilst many of the more traditional manual categories will continue to accelerate the decline which they have experienced in the entire post-war period. Thus, largely inadvertently, the Left has built itself a base where the future action is likely to be. However, it will only be able to build on that base if it first recognizes it and consciously builds upon it, rather than treating its own class composition as a distinct embarrassment which it must constantly deny or quietly ignore, while at the same time engaging in a curious cult of the 'factory gate'.

If it is to build upon its real constituency, the Left must also utilize the characteristic which gives it its greatest appeal amongst these people – its capacity for analysis and coherent argument. For if all the sections of the working class identified as the Left's real (rather than mythical) base have one characteristic in common, it is of course that they are involved in 'mental labour' of various sorts. One is dealing with workers who are nearly always highly literate, sometimes also highly numerate, and very much orientated towards intellectual and creative activities in the widest sense. Sometimes these capacities are used in their formal occupations, more often they are formally required but actually frustrated (often a powerful factor in political radicalization). But in any event they are characteristics which predispose these workers to the kind of rationalist humanitarian politics which, at its best, the Left can offer. This does not mean of course that Left activity can be restricted to writing for intellectual journals. But it does mean that the Left has no reason either to hide or be ashamed of its intellectualism. On the contrary, it needs to improve and hone its arguments and analysis (since if I am right its actual and potential popular base is an extremely critical one) and at the same time present them in persuasive and popular forms. Historically it has been rather bad at the latter task. Left intellectuals in particular often move from abstruse intellectual debate to question-begging demagoguery in one bound with little or nothing in between. The reason for this of course is precisely that lack of class awareness which I noted earlier. One writes one thing for the critical scrutiny of fellow Left intellectuals and something entirely different for 'the working class'. Failure to situate oneself in class terms breeds an élitism, and that élitism in turn breeds demagoguery when the Left is required to 'go popular'. Thus we have the *New Left Review* and *Economy and Society* on the one hand and the *Socialist Worker* and *Militant* on the other. A middle-range

literature which relates Marxist analysis in a popular, comprehensible and intelligent way to current political and policy
issues is still thin on the ground. Very recently, however, there
have been the beginnings of a more hopeful trend in the
emergence and popularity both of the British Communist Party's
revitalized journal *Marxism Today* and of the Labour Party's
New Socialist magazine. The very healthy sales of these journals,
sales which would be even greater, I suspect, if they could obtain
still better access to distribution channels, is a confirmation that
the Left's actual constituency is as I identify it.

It also follows from this analysis that if the Left currently
possesses a popular base in those categories of the working class
which are likely to expand and become dominant in the further
development of capitalism, then socialists have an interest not in
capitalism's collapse in the current crisis, but in its surmounting
that crisis and in its continuing development. Since this is such a
totally heretical position, it is necessary to say something more
about it and in particular about the conception of socialism
which this position implies.

Capitalism has a constant tendency to enlarge the scale of
economic and political activity and to involve human beings in
ever more complex webs of social and economic interdependence
(to 'socialize' production more and more as I shall say). At the
same time, however, it maintains ownership and control of
economic resources in the hands of a tiny minority, principally
through private property. There is therefore a possibility for the
working class to turn this passive 'socialization' of human
activity, brought about through capitalist development, into an
active conscious control, exercised democratically. In other
words, capitalism depends ever more completely upon the
working class with each advance in its productive power because
that power is a product of the interdependent activities of millions
of human beings. But looking at the matter as individuals or as
sectional groups, workers conceive themselves as dependent
upon capitalism, indeed as controlled by 'it' (an entity conceived
as other and alien to them – 'the system') while themselves

exercising little or no control over their own destiny. Moreover, in so far as this is an individual or group conception it is essentially true. As long as workers fail to exercise their power as a class, it is true that the influence they can exercise over capitalism as a total system is minimal. Certain economically crucial groups may have greater capacity than others to wage economistic struggles, but even this power, so long as it is exercised sectionally, is essentially defensive. It can maintain living standards or job security for example, while those of weaker groups are threatened, but it can never in itself transform the passive socialization brought about by capitalism into an active, conscious 'social' control.

Now the point about such a conception of human liberation (about which I shall say more later) is that it requires of workers both imagination and great self-confidence. Imagination to conceive that things could be other than they are and self-confidence to believe that they have the skills and the intelligence to exercise democratic control over economic and social life, and indeed to design the institutions which can make such control effective and compatible with a necessary degree of efficiency and social discipline. Discipline is a particularly important concept here, because Marx's conception of socialism and communism involves nothing less than the substitution of coercive discipline (exercised through fear – of unemployment, of the state, of men, of foreigners) by a voluntary accepted mass self-discipline, based on mutual respect and rational acceptance of the necessity for certain sorts of self-restraint in the general interest.

It is useful sometimes to say these things about the change to a socialist world, if only to be clear as to what, as a socialist, one is actually committed. For these are breathtaking changes. They truly amount to a 'revolutionary' transformation of the world we know and of the world that most human beings have known since the very beginnings of our species. Socialism's enemies see these principles as simply and irredeemably utopian and as bound to degenerate into 'totalitarianism' if any attempt is actually made to create societies on their bases. Obviously I do not hold this view. But I do hold that such a transformation, involving as it does the very fundamentals of human life, is bound to take a very long time indeed. And by a very long time I mean centuries, not years or even decades. Capitalism as a fully fledged form of economy made its first appearance in the world some 200 or so years ago, and I am far from convinced that it has yet exhausted all its potentialities. But whether it has or not, in the life of our planet and indeed of our species, another two or three times that period to get to a socialist world does not seem particularly excessive.

However, let us leave this sort of speculation aside for a moment. If it is true that even to begin such a transformation involves both imagination and self-confidence, one has thereby a criterion, running parallel to the more conventional economistic criterion of the 'development of the productive forces', by which socialists may assess the progressiveness of capitalism. That is, one may say that capitalism is performing a progressive function in the world if it is both developing the productive forces and creating more and more social groups and individuals with both the imagination to conceive of a radically transformed world and the self-confidence to believe in their own ability to exercise democratic control in that world.

Conversely, one may say that one of the effects (not necessarily intended but real nonetheless) of gross class oppression, sexual oppression or racial oppression is both to restrict imagination (so that an alternative sort of world is literally inconceivable) and to undermine self-confidence, so that controlling even one's own life, let alone public institutions, seems a hopeless task. Repeating what I have said before, however, it is dangerous to see such attitudes as purely or even primarily an emanation of 'false consciousness'. They much more often reflect a real situation of individual or group powerlessness, though of course, by inhibiting moves toward wider solidarity, they also reinforce that powerlessness.

It follows, however, that if restriction of imagination and undermining of self-confidence are broadly correlated with the degree of oppression which people undergo, then the most imaginative and self-confident groups and individuals, and thus those most likely to adopt consciously radical positions, may well be those who objectively are the least oppressed. One may even risk a generalization to the effect that consciousness of oppression and the desire to transform the world so as to be rid of oppression are inversely proportional to the 'objective' degree of oppression suffered. Or, in other words, the less oppressed you are, the more you are likely to recognize your oppression as such, i.e. as the product of a humanly created, and thus humanly alterable situation, and not as, for example, 'fate', 'bad luck', or simply 'the way things are'. This must be understood in a purely relative sense, however. I observe, for example, that women who take up consciously feminist positions are often those women who suffer less sexual oppression than women who are not consciously feminist. This does not mean, however, that they suffer no such oppression or that their experience of oppression is simply a product of the over-heated imagination of the privileged. It simply means – what is in fact a sociological commonplace – that if released from certain forms of oppression (through education, contraception, occupational mobility or higher income), one is often more conscious of other forms when one meets them: in occupational discrimination, in interpersonal and intellectual attitudes, in the activities of public and private bureaucracies and so on.

Conversely, the most imaginatively limiting and self-confidence-sapping forms of oppression are often those which are closely related with (but not necessarily reducible to) crude material deprivation. For such deprivation places a premium on simple physical survival and allows little time or energy for wider reflection, either upon oneself or upon society. Moreover, even when the most crippling material constraints have been largely removed (as they have, for example, for most of the male manual 'working class' in Britain), educational limitations, limitations on occupational and social mobility and highly authoritarian family and work experiences can often severely limit both imagination and personal self-confidence. It is one of the most serious shortcomings among traditional Left sects who still orientate their activities strongly to male manual workers, that while they speak often, and rightly, of the oppression and exploitation which the 'working class' (defined in this limited way) suffers, their analysis of this oppression remains extraordinarily banal and contradictory. For while suffering such exploitation, and indeed because they suffer it, such workers are simultaneously predicated by certain groups on the Left with a smouldering revolutionary consciousness which only has to be prodded into life through 'the experience of struggle'. But this simply ignores the possibility (which I think is the actuality) that the forms of exploitation and oppression which the manual 'working class' have suffered historically in Britain have created a class consciousness which is militantly defensive (of what are seen as certain traditional rights and privileges) but which essentially accepts a subordinate position in society provided such rights are respected. This acceptance in turn resides in a deeply rooted sense of inferiority, of which certain forms of cultural class aggressiveness (of speech and manner) are an expression, not a denial. This curious psychological 'set' of the manual 'working class' in Britain (brash aggressiveness cloaking a profound defensiveness and sense of inferiority) is a product of a long and tortured history of class and cultural repression and domination. It is perhaps the most tragic scar of that oppression which the British manual 'working class' wears, far more tragic and horrible in some ways that the worst forms of material poverty, for it is a scarring of the soul and spirit, and is a profoundly conservative force.

But if, however sadly, this is so, then from the point of view of socialists any changes in the economic and occupational structure of capitalism which alter the social composition of the working class (and thus weaken those groups within it who bear these attitudes and values of historical repression most strongly) can only be a progressive change. Especially this is so if the working class is restructured to include far more categories whose education, mobility and lifestyle are likely to endow them both with greater imagination and (above all) self-confidence. I have suggested earlier that such changes have been going on since the Second World War and are likely to accelerate as capitalism restructures itself in crisis. Many of the 'new' white collar and service categories of the working class are likely to come from manual 'working class' backgrounds and especially from the families of skilled manual workers. But there are complex reasons of personal and occupational circumstances why their attitudes and values may be very different.

To argue in this way is to go directly against what is still the traditional Left orthodoxy on this matter which insists that manual 'working class' people in particular must be central to the construction of socialism. Such a view is often based on an essentially cataclysmic view of economic crises in which the sharply worsening situation which manual 'working class' people suffer in such crises gradually forces defensive 'economistic' actions to become more and more militant and eventually to turn into revolutionary struggles. In fact it is only on the basis of this particular theory of crises that one can get from such essentially defensive actions to revolutionary advance at all.

And yet this theory will hardly do. All historical evidence on capitalist crises suggests that they can be as helpful to the Right as to the Left, and in any case, unless one conceives the matter in a total 'big bang' fashion, it is clear that even the most severe capitalist crises affect different groups of workers very unevenly. Sharp increases in unemployment and in the threat of unemployment are as likely to produce general conservatism and a downturn in militancy as its opposite. Convinced monetarists in the Tory party are only evincing the ruling-class candour that used to be commonplace, but is now rather rare, when they assert these 'advantages' of unemployment openly. Moreover, whilst the continuous oscillations of capitalism and its necessarily unstable development make workers very suspicious of its periods of prosperity and inclined to take what they can while it lasts, the very same experience of instability makes for a belief that 'things are bound to get better' even amidst the worst slump. Far from being a vacuous optimism, I believe that such expectations are rational and well founded, but once again their political effect (combined with minimal social security provisions) is to produce a determination to 'sit it out' in a rather passive fashion whilst taking one's revenge at the ballot box on any government which is in power at the time. The very cyclical nature then of capitalist crises makes their net effect distinctly conservative. But, to return to my former point, I believe that this is so because in Britain in particular such crises act upon a class whose historical formation has drained it of the necessary self-confidence and imagination which would make it possible to see capitalist crises as opportunities: opportunities for socialist transformation or the beginnings of such transformation. This is the missing factor – the crucial intervening term – required to turn capitalist crises (and their accompanying assaults on living standards) into revolutionary situations. It is a missing term continually ignored or wished away by the traditional Left, implicitly, I think, in the belief that 'if things get bad enough' this problem will somehow take care of itself. But this is a chimera. There are very good theoretical reasons for believing that crises can never get that bad (i.e. part of the function of crises under capitalism is to produce the means of their own cessation, albeit at immense social cost). And even if, for the sake of argument, we allow that things might get that bad (and imagine, for example, a situation in which 80 per cent of all workers were permanently unemployed and destitute), it is not clear that the Left would be the primary beneficiary of such a situation. In a moment where the choice was clearly and unambiguously between socialism and barbarism, would one bet against barbarism?

So, in short, a particular, defensive and conservative form of class consciousness is a prime impediment to socialist transformation in Britain, and indeed in many other parts of the advanced capitalist world. The strength of this impediment, this blockage, is most clearly revealed at moments of capitalist crisis such as we are now experiencing, moments which in traditional theory 'ought' to be moments of unparalleled opportunity for the Left.

However, this consciousness tends to weaken as the occupational and social structure of the working class changes, and in particular as the traditional manual 'working class' declines and the class as a whole has a greater weight of more highly educated service occupations. However, such shifts are slow and uneven, and above all require prolonged periods of capitalist boom. It follows that the central task of the Left in the current situation is to help restore boom conditions as quickly as possible, but to do so in ways which, whilst simultaneously helping capital to restructure itself, also provide real political and economic gains for the working class. In Chapter 5 I suggest how this might be done.

Socialism

Since this chapter and all the ones which follow are based in one way or another on the idea that advances towards socialism occur most frequently in periods of high and rising material prosperity and not in conditions either of gross material deprivation or of slump or crisis, it is necessary now to focus on this idea. I want especially to distinguish between the activities of self-consciously socialist individuals and groups and the activities of others. For I shall argue that individuals and groups who are self-consciously socialist may act in ways which actually damage the prospects of advance towards socialism, whilst non-socialist groups and individuals may act in ways which actually aid such advance although they are motivated by quite different goals and objectives.

In clarifying this issue and providing a criterion of advance towards (or retrogression from) socialism, I found a quotation from the nineteenth-century Russian thinker Mikhailovsky very useful. It is useful not for its substantive content, with which I entirely disagree, but for its linguistic and logical form, which I have borrowed and turned to my own purposes. In his article 'What is Progress?' (1869), Mikhailovsky said

> Progress is the gradual approach to the integral individual, to the fullest possible and the most diversified division of labour

among man's organs and the least possible division of labour among men. Everything that impedes this advance is immoral, unjust, pernicious and unreasonable. Everything that diminishes the heterogeneity of society, and thereby increases the heterogeneity of its members is moral, just, reasonable and beneficial.

Similarly, I wish to ask 'What is Socialism?' and to reply:

Socialism is the greatest possible degree of conscious human control over the personal, social and natural environment exercised democratically. Everything that impedes advance towards such control is immoral, unjust, pernicious and unreasonable and a retrogression from socialism. Everything that advances such control and its democratic exercise is moral, just, reasonable and beneficial, and an advance towards socialism.

It will be seen that this criterion (the Mikhailovsky/Kitching criterion, or M/K criterion as I shall refer to it subsequently) is not free from ambiguity. First, what constitutes increased conscious human control over the personal, social (where social includes economic) and natural environment must to a large degree be a matter of judgement in particular cases. As I hope to show, the actual scope for disagreement here is smaller than might appear. Second, and more seriously, the criterion is double-barrelled. It is in fact two criteria incorporating (a) conscious human control over the total environment and (b) the democratic exercise of that control. Clearly (b) does not necessarily follow from (a): one may have increased control over some aspect of the environment without such control being exercised democratically. More importantly still, it is arguable that some forms of control over the environment cannot by their very nature be exercised democratically (since perhaps they require specialist expertise or knowledge not universally available). Clearly, this is not an issue which can be resolved in general terms, but must be investigated and struggled over from case to case. In any event, a socialist advance would, on the M/K criterion, occur when there was some increase of human control in some given area and/or in its democratic exercise. Socialist advance consists of a continuous 'testing' of the limits both of such control and of its democratic exercise, and these limits may themselves vary historically with technological change and rising educational standards.

In the light of the M/K criterion I may now make somewhat more exact the meaning of my earlier statement that advances toward socialism are more likely to occur in periods of capitalist boom. First, increases in the productivity of human labour and growth of the productive forces in conditions of long boom generally entail some increase in conscious human control over the natural environment. However, such control is usually not exercised democratically (on the contrary it is usually concentrated in a fairly narrow managerial and scientific stratum).

Second, and more importantly, it is my contention that during capitalist booms more and more strata and groups become functionally necessary to the effective exercise of capitalist control over the social and natural environment, whilst themselves becoming painfully aware that such control is not exercised democratically. While fulfilling important ancillary roles, such groups exercise little or no control over the institutions in which they are involved. Third, and most vitally of all, the expansion of capitalism under boom conditions continually expands the scale of enterprise, making ever more complex and interdependent the social division of labour, and rendering the whole system more and more dependent on the interlocking activities of millions of human beings whilst at the same time denying the majority of these people any influence or control over the environments in which they live and work. At the same time, by reliance on 'market forces', the capitalist system renders the total social and natural environment outside the control of anyone (including the capitalists themselves).* Thus the paradox which is at the heart of

* This is a point worth stressing. Much socialist propaganda in this country and elsewhere tends to leave the impression that the prime socialist objection to capitalism is that it is a 'class' system run and controlled by a minority (the capitalist class) in their interests and at the expense of the majority. However, this

capitalism, between ever-increasing rationality, bureaucratization and control at the sectoral level or the level of the individual
firm, and an uncontrollable instability at the macro level (at the
level of total employment, or the total output mix, or total energy
consumption). Hence too, the tension experienced at all levels of
the capitalist system from the lives of individuals to the destinies
of multi-national corporations and governments, between an
ever-growing socialization, bureaucratization and control at one
level, and a sense of total chaos, instability and unpredictability
at another. It is this contradiction, identified a century or more
ago by Marx, which lies at the heart of the capitalist system and
which socialism must resolve or at least ameliorate. However,
such a resolution requires the presence of individuals and groups
who are aware of this contradiction in their daily lives and who
feel confident that they can overcome it or ameliorate it by the
extension of conscious social control over the total (macro-level)
environment. This control would grow from advances in the
democratic control of existing institutions (individual firms and
organizations, national and local governments) and the creation
of new institutions of democratic control at local, national and
international levels. I have argued above that certain 'new'
sections of the working class may be in personal, social and
occupational situations which both heighten the awareness of
contradiction and breed self-confidence in their capacity to
overcome it or ameliorate it in political and public ways by the
extension of democratic control.

It is not difficult to see the varying forms which such public
activity can take. They include (a) attempts to protect the natural

---

was certainly not Marx's fundamental objection to capitalism, which was a far
more powerful and telling one. His major criticism of capitalism was that as a
total system it was not controlled by anyone, including the capitalists. For this
reason the major task for socialism was to substitute for the violently unstable
forms of control exercised over capitalism by 'market forces', a consciously
organized and democratic control exercised by all producers and consumers
together. The question is, however, whether this is feasible in reality, and if so,
how.

environment or the social and residential environment from certain forms of industrial or commercial development, or to insist that such development is done with a concern for the environment even if at greater financial cost; (b) protest movements against new road schemes; (c) trade union and worker protest against dangerous working conditions and support for stricter controls over such conditions; (d) consumer movements of all types; (e) attempts to enforce a higher standard of health care and to produce a healthier natural and social environment. All these movements in one way or another aim to expand the degree of human control over the environment. They aim, in different ways, to make the total 'living environment' one which is determined by human beings in general, rather than being under the control of small élites, or what is perhaps worse, under nobody's control at all. All such movements expand the realm of public debate and action by widening the range of concerns and issues deemed suitable for such action. In societies which also have strong counter pressures toward privatization (see pp. 34–5), such movements represent the reassertion of old 'republican' virtues, of the concept of a truly human life as a public as well as a private life in which a citizen has duties as well as rights, and in which the performance of civic duties is the primary safeguard of liberty. This civic ideal, born in Periclean Athens, beloved of the Machiavelli of *The Discourses* and reasserted by Rousseau, exercised a profound influence on Marx (who after all began life as a classical scholar) and is, in my view, at the heart of his fragmentary vision of the communist society.

So then the M/K criterion embraces as socialist or as contributing to the construction of a socialist world a whole variety of social movements and demands, many of which are not dominated by self-conscious socialists and some of which involve people whose conscious attitude to socialism might very well be hostile. It also suggests precisely why I argued earlier that socialist advance defined in this way is more likely to occur, and does in fact occur most pronouncedly in capitalist booms, or at least in periods of 'full employment' and constantly rising living standards. For in such periods the number of people and of social groups 'released' from the narrowing dictates of economic survival and able to devote time and energy to public and social concerns grows rapidly. In short, in a very general sense, in capitalist long booms society becomes increasingly 'politicized', or at least (for the matter is contradictory) certain groups and strata become increasingly politicized, while others may remain profoundly de-politicized or may indeed become more de-politicized.

This latter reflection on which I now wish to expand means that my earlier assertion that socialist construction needs capitalist booms must be understood only in a highly qualified and long-term sense. For the effect of boom conditions on political and social consciousness depends mainly on the social and historical background of the group of people affected. Broadly speaking, people who enter long boom conditions with a background of absolute or relative material deprivation are likely, under boom conditions, to turn increasingly to a highly privatized form of material consumption. They enjoy as 'the good life' forms and types of consumption which do indeed represent a real improvement in the quality of life for such groups (I would not wish to echo some socialists' contempt for such consumption) and which have been denied to them and their parents and grandparents earlier. However, people who enter long booms when they are already relatively affluent are quite likely to generate from their ranks the most ardent converts to 'anti-materialist' movements and philosophies, some (not all) of which may lead on to public and political activism. Conversely, groups who had previously responded to material deprivation by certain sorts of (mainly economistic) 'militancy' may become much more de-politicized with affluence. However, in all cases, it changes with the generations, and one may risk the generalization that the longer such material affluence lasts, the less likely it is – provided boom conditions continue – to be of great personal or social importance for the group or strata involved.

However, even if there is, as I would argue, a tendency for anti-materialist sentiments to grow in significance with material affluence, such sentiments are by no means necessarily linked with public activism. Indeed, the experience in the United States shows clearly that such sentiments can often take mystical or quietist forms of a highly 'personalist' sort. The more affluent sections of American society have spawned a whole variety of religious or quasi-religious creeds whose believers seek happiness in purely personal changes of some sort. Very many of these creeds, interestingly, rest on the same extreme idealism which counsels that nothing is a problem if one does not think or feel that it is. All that differentiates these creeds is the means recommended to bring about such changes in thought and feeling, from a variety of psychological and social psychological recipes, through prayer and meditation, to drugs.

Nothing may be more reactionary than such quietism, whatever form it takes, counselling as it does, withdrawal from all public and social concerns (as 'corrupt' or corrupting and/or hopeless) and leaving the public and political domain to the dominance of some of the most opportunistic and corrupt sections of the American ruling class. But aside from this kind of active de-politicization produced by booms, it is clear that even many of the groups and movements who under the M/K criterion I have identified as marking advances to socialist construction are hardly unproblematic. For a start, a number of them are highly élitist or divisive. 'Middle class' opposition to road schemes evaporates when the roads are re-routed through a 'working class' estate. Opposition to industrial or commercial developments is often very similarly sectional. 'Consumer groups' very often mobilize from the more affluent consumers, who can afford to be discriminating about what they buy. Both racial and sexual liberation movements can have exclusivist tendencies (see Chapter 4 on feminism for a discussion of this issue), and as a result fail even to mobilize most of their self-identified constituency whilst alienating potential allies outside it.

All this is true. But its implication is only that this kind of public and political ferment must be more widely generalized if it is to be actually, rather than ambiguously, democratic. 'Middle class' protest and consumer groups should have to contend with 'working class' protest and consumer groups, as well as with public authorities and capitalists vending goods and services. Both racial and sexual liberation movements must be confronted by sympathetic groups of whites, blacks, browns, heterosexuals and men, who have the confidence both to identify with what they find valid and to challenge what they find partial or false. It is my contention only that the possibilities for the generalization of this ferment are more propitious in times of capitalist long booms than they are in times of recession or slump. For, during slumps, there is frequently a widespread (though fortunately by no means total) retreat into the protection of personal and group material interests very narrowly conceived (job security, income mainten-ance, etc.). Such a retreat may indeed be marked by quite 'militant' public activity (strikes, demonstrations, etc.), but this should not lead the Left to mistake its essential character of retreat and retrenchment. Only old demands, never new ones, are made in slumps. They are very rarely, if at all, times of advances.

One needs, I think, to take this point further into examination of historical cases. For it might seem possible to refute this generalization easily by reference to a host of historical examples. Did not the first mass socialist movement in the world – the Chartist movement – emerge at a period of slump? Were not the most radical and revolutionary years in the history of this century (the period between 1917 and 1921) years of acute economic depression after the First World War? And what about the radicalization and political polarization produced by the 1930s depression?

I hope it will be seen that such counter-examples are not in fact counter-examples to the generalization I am offering. For whilst mass movements of the distressed have often been led by socialists and revolutionaries, I am arguing here that it was precisely the motivation of their mass base which rendered them fatally flawed as socialist movements. If, irrespective of the ideologies of their leaders, the mass support for revolutionary movements is born of desperation induced by extreme material deprivation, then when the deprivation diminishes, so does the desperation and along with it the mass support for radical change. There are also more fundamental problems for revolutionary movements made up overwhelmingly of poor people, especially in the 'post-revolutionary' situation, and I shall discuss these more fully in Chapter 2. Here I want simply to say that in the idea of socialism which I am offering, the strength of socialist movements is to be measured by the extent to which they are composed of people who cannot be 'bought off' by material improvements in their standard of living, because they do not enter such movements in the first place primarily in order to obtain such improvements. And conversely, I am arguing that all socialist movements in the past have been crucially weakened by the essentially limited objectives of their mass following (as distinct from parts at least of their leaderships), objectives which were subsequently 'discovered' to be fulfillable within capitalism, given continued capitalist development.

However, periods of long boom and rising material prosperity are at best propitious periods for struggle. Nothing is inevitable. All is to be won. Moreover, even if world capitalism should survive the current crisis and prosper again, the distance still to be traversed in the struggle for socialist transformation remains enormous. For the kind of democratic control over the environment which I identified in embryo in the movements enumerated above has still barely touched the real centres of economic and social decision-making in individual capitalist nations. Moreover, it is totally absent at an international level, although capitalism itself has become more and more a world-wide system. Yet in the end democratic control over the natural, economic, social and personal environment will involve encroachments on these central powers – on the power to decide what is to be produced, how it is to be produced and distributed, and where such production and distribution are to take place. Such powers are the crucial ones in the capitalist economic system, and indeed in any economic system. The transfer of such powers from small minorities (whether these be capitalist owners and managers or 'central planners' in state socialism) to the majority of the population is not to be achieved without widespread social and political conflict (some of it, probably, involving violence), even if it is conceived, as I conceive it, as necessarily an extremely gradual process. To that extent, then, I remain a very old-fashioned Marxist, believing very firmly that socialist transformation does involve class and sectional 'struggle' of a real and sometimes nasty sort. My only quarrel with conventional Marxism is with who is conceived as the 'working class' engaged in this struggle. In particular, the concepts that determine which workers are regarded as the 'vanguard' in this struggle are, to my mind, static and outmoded – and they have been made outmoded precisely by developments in contemporary capitalism.

Democracy

There is another and even more difficult side to all this, which involves the second aspect of the M/K criterion: the issue of democratic control over 'environmental' (in the widest sense) decision-making. It needs to be said quite frankly that this is the weakest element in socialist theory of all types. For we have only the vaguest and most unsatisfactory ideas about how it might be converted from a slogan to reality. Marx's own response to this problem, insofar as he had any at all, was simply to leave the matter to be solved by 'practice' in the transition first to socialism and then to communism. Such a solution has a strand of common sense, for it is obvious that actual situations are so complex and varied that a process of 'trial and error' in building the necessary institutions has to play a part in any real situation. To that degree detailed 'blueprints' are neither feasible nor helpful, particularly if we conceive all such transitions in long timespans of centuries. But this can hardly be a complete answer, since it is clear from historical experience that certain, very severe, structural problems are involved here, which recur time and time again whenever any attempt is made to democratize economic and social decision-making. The central structural difficulty is that the more democratic and open any decision-making process is, the longer it takes. However, even in the most meticulously planned environments many decisions have to be taken in reponse to rapidly changing situations and cannot, except at the cost of total stasis and chaos, be 'left' until a highly democratic decision-making process has been completed. Almost immediately then, in any real situation it becomes necessary to delegate powers from larger, more democratic bodies (be these workers' and peasant assemblies or whatever) to smaller, more 'efficient' bodies. However, once such delegation has occurred, a great deal of the real day-to-day decision-making power is taken out of democratic channels and placed in the hands of small minorities which may then be beyond the effective control of the larger bodies. This problem becomes particularly acute if it is desired to replace market determinants of resource use by 'planned' (i.e. consciously co-ordinated and controlled) decision-making. For if the economy and society involved are at all complex (and the classical Marxist conception of transition to socialism from advanced capitalism presupposes that they would be), the decision-making and planning process is of inordinate complexity, especially if it is done 'centrally'. Attempts to combine such decision-making with genuinely democratic forms of information dissemination and decision-taking threaten to make the economic system totally unworkable and to result in its effective breakdown as a system for producing and distributing goods and services. But the generalization of want, on however democratic a basis, is hardly an advance on capitalism. Most people would, quite sensibly it seems to me, sacrifice a mountain of democracy for a reliable supply of bread.

But this is not all. The harsh fact is that socialists have little or no idea how it even might be possible to exercise genuinely democratic control over the vast range of social and economic institutions at a local, national and international level, which are currently involved in the complex functioning of modern capitalist societies and of the world capitalist system as a whole. In particular, a persistent and apparently insoluble tension exists between the centralizing tendencies which seem to be inherent in the desire to substitute planned control at macro levels for the market forces which determine these macro outcomes under capitalism, and the apparent need to make economic and social decision-making under socialism much more decentralized and small scale in nature if it is to have any hope at all of being genuinely democratic and 'unalienated'.

The growth of capitalism as a genuinely world-wide system of production has even produced assertions by some socialists that socialism on a national basis is impossible now and can only be realized along with 'world government'. Marx himself is no help at all with this dilemma, since he seemed to regard a 'social' (i.e. universal and democratic) control of total production and consumption – and the exercise of that control in a highly decentralized and small-scale fashion – as unproblematically complementary without ever suggesting how, exactly, this could be. Some socialist theorists have, very speculatively, seen the resolution of this contradiction in certain 'new technologies' of production and distribution now emerging which would simultaneously expand output and consumption whilst reducing the size of production units (and thus the necessary size of residential areas). More conventional debate on these issues has usually revolved around the forms and degree of decentralization of decision-making which may be compatible with a centrally 'planned' economy. In this debate some writers have suggested that the partial reintroduction of the 'market principle' into socialism may be necessary, both in the interests of economic efficiency and (as in Yugoslavia, for example) with the aim of making worker and community control over economic enterprises a real, rather than formal, reality. In Yugoslavia, however, the problem has been that the total reintroduction of market competition between enterprises has brought with it some of the consequences which appear in capitalist market economies – especially sharp increases in income inequalities among workers and among regions and growing unemployment.

These issues are far too complex and wide-ranging to be discussed adequately in a book primarily addressed to other issues, but I will provocatively – and simply – present as assertions some ideas which need at least to be faced and elaborated if the process of socialist construction is to make any practical progress.

(1) Under any currently known technology and (despite speculation) under any technology which is likely to become available in the foreseeable future, there *is* an insoluble contradiction between the desire to exert a planned, conscious control over what is produced, how it is produced, and how it is distributed and consumed, and the desire to maintain all such decisions at a level of scale and locality that they can be exercised democratically by all producers and consumers in society. This being the case, some important economic decisions must, under socialism, be delegated to smaller groups of higher level decision-makers. It therefore follows that the construction of democratic institutions through which such decision-makers can be popularly monitored, and, if necessary, replaced, is of paramount importance in the construction of socialism. This in turn means that such issues as access to information (about what the decision-makers are doing and why), democratic forms of election of decision-makers, and questions of their real and formal responsibility to more democratic institutions become absolutely central. The failure of the Bolsheviks to pay any attention at all to this 'constitutionalist' side of socialism was one (but just one, and not historically the most important) root of the decline of Russian socialism into despotism. Taking these constitutionalist issues seriously and constructing institutions through which the socialist state can be more constitutionally democratic than the capitalist state is what was meant in classical Marxism by the assertion that socialism must maintain and cherish but also 'go beyond' bourgeois–democratic political forms. The constitutional 'checks and balances' which conventional political theory holds dear are no mere 'ideological mystifications' to be swept aside in socialist revolution. In their actual practice (in the US and elsewhere) their effect is weakened and at times totally

negated by the exercise of class power under capitalism. Yet at
the same time they act as a powerful ideological legitimation of
that power because they have a limited but real effectiveness
(witness both the fate of Richard Nixon and the powerful
ideological vindication of the American system into which his
ejection was turned). The task for socialists is to make that
effectiveness greater by the design of more powerful and
democratic institutions for the exercise and control of state
power freed from class domination. Construction of such
effective checks and balances becomes even more important
when the executive and administrative power of the state is
increased by the accretion of new economic functions under
socialism.

(2) It seems clear, from the experience of central planning in the
Soviet Union and eastern Europe, that a market mechanism must
play a central economic role in democratic socialism. It seems the
only effective way to match the use of resources to their relative
scarcity, to guarantee a real degree of consumer choice and power
and to provide for real worker and community controls over
enterprises. This however does not entail the re-introduction of
private property (or its maintenance) since the enterprises may be
co-operative or collective units of various sizes. However, I at
least see no objection to the maintenance of private ownership of
very small production and service enterprises.*

(3) Under such circumstances, the crucial issue becomes one of
deciding which areas of economic and social activity should be
centrally planned and controlled and which should remain within
the sphere of the market. Although this boundary would
undoubtedly shift for both historical and pragmatic reasons, I
would favour the application of a broad 'social welfare' principle

* For an argument in favour of market socialism, but with a strong directing state,
which seems, at least in its essentials, to be unanswerable, see Alec Nove, *The
Economics of Feasible Socialism*, London, Allen & Unwin, 1983. See also Jim
Tomlinson, *The Unequal Struggle? British Socialism and the Capitalist Enterprise*, London, Methuen, 1982, for an argument starting from a different point but
ending with much the same conclusions.

in drawing the line. This is, 'society' (through the most democratically feasible decision-making process) would identify a 'bundle' of goods and services to which access should be on the basis of need, not discretionary want. All goods and services falling into this category, together with all the inputs and raw materials required to produce them, would be allocated to 'socially controlled' sector under state control. Obvious candidates for inclusion would be health and education services, housing, domestic heat and light, transport, and at least 'basic' food and clothing. All goods and services falling outside this sector could be produced and distributed on a market principle. The aim of the socially controlled sector would be to produce and distribute its goods and services (and their necessary inputs) as cheaply as possible. This could be done either by highly subsidized prices or through 'free' distribution, i.e. these goods and services being paid for out of universally levied taxes. There would undoubtedly be some complications in this division, especially those deriving from substitutable goods and services being produced in the state controlled sector and in the market sector, and raw materials and other inputs which were 'joint products' used in a variety of different industries (some in the state controlled sector and some outside). However, such conflicts would have to be resolved pragmatically and on the principle that it is the interests of the citizens as producers and consumers which should have first priority, not those of the state as an economic unit.

(4) I believe that competition for control of the state decision-making roles would have to be an essential part of a democratic socialist society and that this competition would need to be regularized in competing political parties with competing socialist programmes. These programmes could vary over the size and role of the state controlled sector and the market sector and policies to be applied in each, over 'social policies' of all types, over foreign policy issues, etc. Competition between parties would issue in periodic elections, though this would not be the only means of controlling or replacing state functionaries.

So much for blueprints. The details of this one are all open to dispute, and the actual risk of constructing state economic and social institutions so that they can combine the maximum possible degree of planned and conscious control with the maximum possible degree of democratic control will be a long, complex and shifting process in which popular effort, knowledge and innovativeness will be a lot more important than broad schemes. But the most important thing to say about all this is that it would involve a citizenry of the greatest knowledge, sophistication and self-discipline. And it is the latter that I would wish to stress most. For a world without bosses, a world where executive managers in enterprises and planning functionaries in government are in fact (rather than formally) 'the servants of the people' – trusted representatives given certain clearly delimited and controlled functions for defined periods of time – is necessarily a world in which discipline is self-imposed. It can certainly not be a world without discipline, because in any form of social and economic organization there is a need for certain rules and for sacrifice by some for the benefit of others. Consider for example the situation where in order to free building materials for house construction it has been decided to cut back on the construction of recreation facilities for a given period. A socialist society, on my definition, would be one in which (a) the people who would have used and benefited from those facilities would have taken some part in the decision to do without them, and (b) having been party to that decision would then accept it 'in the general interest'. One could multiply this example a hundred or a thousand times to involve workers foregoing wage increases in order to improve local pension schemes or welfare programmes or the long-term productivity and growth of their enterprises, communities reducing consumption of food to help needier neighbours or others 'abroad', etc. In all cases, the same double rule would have to apply: (a) involvement in the decision, and (b) acceptance of that decision and its attendant costs.

A working class which was able to exercise that degree of self-discipline would 'automatically' also be a working class knowledgeable enough, critical enough, and publicly active enough actually to enforce the responsibilities of their representatives by mass-level scrutiny, criticism and where necessary, popularly enforced recall and re-selection. It was the absence of a 'proletariat' so equipped which produced the problem of 'substitutionism' in the USSR in the early days of the revolution. In the effective absence of a proletariat or citizenry equipped to act as a 'ruling class', it became necessary first to substitute a political party for the class and then (given precisely the same problems at the mass level in the party) to substitute a group of leaders, and finally, a single leader for the party. The sophisticated rationalizations which the Bolsheviks offered for the initial substitution (of party for class) and the intricacies of the power struggle which eventually produced a single man's tyranny out of party control should not blind us to the fact that that initial, and fatal, substitution was essentially forced on the Bolshevik party by the absence of a proletariat equipped to exercise such democratic control. Since I hold that the production of such a proletariat may take centuries of capitalist development, its effective absence in 1917 (not only in Russia but, I would argue, anywhere else in the world) is hardly surprising. The slow but determined self-construction of such a class is the primary socialist task within capitalism.

Conclusions

A socialist world then must necessarily be a world very different from the one we know, a world permeated at every level with what the ancient Athenians called the principle of 'civic virtue', where citizens' duties are stressed as much as their rights – and indeed, in which the performance of such duties is an important safeguard of rights. In a socialist world, however, it may be possible actually to operate this principle, because with the abolition of private property and minority control, decisions taken in the 'general interest' really are in that interest and not in some disguised class interest. It is also possible if material productivity is so high and the working week so short that the majority of the citizens' waking hours can be used for public (as well as private) activities.

It may now be evident why I think that such changes will take a very long time to occur and will be gradual in their emergence, even if not always peaceful. I also think that it is hopelessly naive to expect that such 'virtues' (as the ancients called them) can be systematically neglected under capitalism and then 'suddenly' emerge on the day or hour of socialist revolution. I therefore hold that the struggle for socialism under capitalism should concentrate on any and all issues which expand popular control over the environment together with the democratic exercise of that control, and that a collective sense of responsibility and self-discipline should be built. Obviously these two dimensions are interlinked. Nobody ever learnt a sense of responsibility or about the complexity of the world and of the need for self-discipline whilst remaining powerless. Indeed, one of the few 'benefits' of being totally powerless is that one can afford to be irresponsible: there is simply no pressure on one to cease believing that all things are possible. We see this manifested perfectly in the behaviour of the British electorate and indeed in the behaviour of all other western electorates who continually demand of their politicians in power that they achieve mutually incompatible objectives simultaneously (e.g. lower inflation and full employment, higher wages and lower prices, better public services and lower taxes). In conditions of crisis, politicians in western democracies fall prey to such electorates in ever more frequent and violent electoral 'swings', but at the same time they continue to encourage such irresponsibility (through competitive bidding in unrealistic promises) because this is the price (a price most of them are very willing to pay) to keep the ignorant and powerless majority as it is – ignorant because powerless and powerless because ignorant. Socialists should demand more power for the people, under capitalism, both because as such power expands it continually tests the democratic limits of capitalism *qua* capitalism, and also because only through the exercise of power, or involvement in campaigns to effect its exercise, can a working class be created capable of running a socialist society. Indeed, only in this way would a working class be able to conceive and believe that it could take the responsibility for running anything.

2 / Socialism and underdevelopment

In the introduction to this book I argued that it is impossible to construct meaningfully democratic societies (whether socialist or not) in materially poor societies. In this chapter I shall try to demonstrate what I meant by this, and having demonstrated it, to draw some more general conclusions from it.

The argument itself has two sides to it. In the first place it refers to the material and social conditions of the majority of the people in poor countries which act as a powerful impediment to their playing a full part, as active citizens, in their own societies. The points to be made here are commonplace enough and need not detain us long. The second side of the argument is perhaps a little less commonplace but in my view is of immense importance, especially in socialist societies in the Third World. It concerns the attitudes and values of those who enter public life and, in particular, of those who occupy public office in such societies.

To take the first part first. It is commonly observed by those who have lived in and studied a variety of countries in the Third World that the bulk of the population in such countries play a marginal or largely passive role in their politics. In some, of course (especially those under military rule), there are no popular elections to office so that even this restricted form of political involvement is denied to the bulk of the population. In yet other countries (both communist and non-communist) some form of one-party state exists so that general elections are a quasi-compulsory means of endorsing the regimes in question. Thus, except in one rather extraordinary case (that of Tanzania), their results are little or no guide to the popularity or otherwise of the regimes. In other Third World countries, of which India is the most outstanding example, there is a competitive party system and elections can and do bring about important changes in political power. But the use of power and patronage in the countryside often means that votes are won for local and national party machines through a varied combination of coercion and bribery. Under certain circumstances this can give the poor a degree of leverage: they may 'sell' their votes for certain material or social gains (the provision of a local road, dispensary or other facility, or changes in crop prices or rent levels). But voting is often based on the most minimal understanding either of party ideologies or of national political issues.

Though individual situations are enormously varied, the same broad factors recur again and again in explanations of this popular inertia, particularly in societies still dominated by rural and peasant people. Virtually all sources talk of the need of such people to bend both physical and intellectual efforts either to mere survival or to the attainment of a minimal degree of security and upward mobility in a sea of poverty. To that must be added the effect of constant ill health and disease (affecting both physical and mental energy and performance), the high levels of illiteracy (particularly among women), and the physical and social isolation in which peasants often live. The effect of the latter is not necessarily, in the days of mass media and the ubiquitous transistor radio, to isolate peasants from news and information about national issues. Rather, by narrowing their experience and knowledge, it often renders them incapable of interpreting or even understanding the information to which they are exposed. These kinds of incapacities and disabilities are often present too, though not to the same extent, among urban poor people.

One should be clear about the precise nature of the political inertia or more exactly, incapacity, about which one is speaking here. It certainly does not lie in poor people being totally marginal to the political process in their societies. On the contrary, from time to time they can 'intervene' in the processes in a powerful, even explosive fashion. The 'peasant wars' of liberation in China, Algeria, Mozambique, Angola and Vietnam were only the most spectacular of such interventions, along with the less spectacular anti-colonial nationalist movements of India, Africa and South-East Asia. However, though peasants are often mobilizable for anti-colonial and revolutionary struggles, they are usually mobilized by forces outside the peasantry – often urban-based intellectuals of various types – though some of these people may have a peasant origin. Religion has been and remains a powerful mobilizing force among peasants in certain societies, notably Islamic societies, though once again urban-based priests and others are often the leaders of such movements.

However, such explosive mass interventions in the political process are, by definition, occasional. And once they have occurred, the factors which have often played a part in that mobilization in the first place – poverty, illiteracy, disease, isolation – reassert themselves to prevent – and this is the point – the mass of the citizenry of such countries exercising any effective or continuous oversight or control over the day-to-day decision-making process, certainly at a national level, in their own societies. Of course, in many Third World societies which are dictatorships of one sort or another there is no constitutional way in which they could do this anyway. But even in societies where it is constitutionally possible, material factors keep this possibility purely formal for the vast majority of its citizenry. It is well known, for example, that in India the effective active citizenry is a small part of the total adult population and is drawn overwhelmingly from the well-off, or at least from the not-so-poor people of that society. The absence of effective resistance to the military coups which frequently replace elected governments in the Third World is also partly due to the kind of factors discussed above.

Peasants and other people are capable, as the example of China shows most clearly, of exercising an effective and continuous oversight of local issues, issues immediately within their experience and essential to their interest (such as decisions on agriculture or land improvement). But even here, this real local-level popular participation is not matched by any popular involvement in national-level decision-making or indeed in national-level leadership questions. The cabalistic politics of a tiny élite which determined the succession in China after the death of Mao Tse-Tung, and in a fashion very similar to the court intrigues of the old Chinese Empire, is perhaps the clearest recent indication of this.

The history of the Bolshevik revolution of 1917 is the most painful and tragic, and certainly the best-known historical case of what occurs in a situation where a revolution is declared in the name of a popular force (the Russian working class) which from the first was a tiny proportion of the total population, was all but wiped out in the war and civil war which followed, and was effectively incapable in any case of exercising the power which had been claimed for it. In such a situation a tiny ruling party exercised power in its name, at first 'temporarily' (while waiting for a European-wide revolution) and eventually permanently. This 'model', originally forced on the Bolsheviks by historical circumstances, later under the Comintern became hallowed as 'democratic-centralism' and 'Marxist-Leninism'. In that form it has been reproduced in China, Vietnam, North Korea, Cuba, Mozambique and Angola, as well as in eastern Europe. In all these cases there is effectively no constitutional control over the party or state exercised by the peasants or workers for whom the party claims to rule. Instead, discipline within the party, and indeed the use of party and state power for ends other than personal enrichment, depend upon the maintenance of self-discipline among both leaders and other party 'cadres'. This self-discipline depends in turn almost entirely upon ideological commitment to a revolutionary ethic of service – to 'the people', 'the revolution', etc.

And this brings us to the second dimension of my original proposition. For both socialist and capitalist societies in the Third World have been, and are, plagued with a continual problem in the exercise of public office. That problem generally goes under the title of 'corruption', but this somewhat ethnocentric description masks a much deeper and broader problem. That problem, to put it simply, is that in very many poor societies across the world it is considered normal and even inevitable that public office should be used for private gain, and indeed that it is not worth acquiring if it cannot be so used. For in many Third World societies, employment in the public service represents an important avenue, and sometimes even the only avenue, to upward social and economic mobility, both for the person who acquires such employment and for his or her family and other dependents. This is the situation all over Africa (in societies nominally capitalist and socialist) and is widespread in other Third World societies as well. Its general effect is to make the use of public power subject to a fairly crude and direct economic imperative. In such societies ideology, in so far as it ever has any hold on the political process (perhaps in the form of a vague populist nationalism), very quickly degenerates into rapid, cynical and consciously manipulated 'rhetoric'. Rhetorical declamations of loyalty and opposition are, and are widely recognized to be, the thinnest and most cynical of covers for personal ambition and greed. Hence the general contempt into which politicians quickly sink among the minority familiar with public life and the vulnerability of many Third World regimes to 'house-cleaning' military coups, the resulting military governments, however, quickly degenerating in the same way.

Socialist and communist regimes in the Third World attempt to defend themselves from such degeneration by the use of an ascetic ethic of revolutionary service to the people, and to a degree both in the early days of the USSR and in the Third World since, this form of antidote or inoculation has been moderately successful, at least among the top leadership. But at lower and lower levels in the bureaucracy and public service (which in a socialist society provides a very high proportion of total employment) it is harder and harder to inculcate or enforce such an ethic. For as the state and economy develops one must draw continually on fresh 'cadres' who may not have been exposed to much, if any, communist or socialist education, or may simply have ignored it if they have. At these levels, it is very hard to avoid the mass infiltration of people who are usually referred to as 'opportunists', but who are often just rather typical representatives of the 'peasants' and 'workers' for whom the revolution was supposedly made. Peasants and workers coming out of poverty are not as a rule (though there are significant and extraordinary exceptions) interested in public office unless they can use it to cease being a peasant or worker, i.e. to cease being poor. Since it is the mass of such middle level and lower cadres whom the mass of the citizens encounter in the actual functioning of the state and 'socialism', this bureaucratic behaviour can quickly produce mass cynicism even if (in the extraordinary psychology of these things), it is fully 'understood' by millions of people in these societies who would themselves do the same thing if they could.

Since this is a very sensitive issue, it is incumbent upon me to express my value judgements here. The revolutionary asceticism which so distinguished Lenin and many of the old Bolsheviks and Mao Tse-Tung and many of his closest collaborators in China is, in my view, something to be profoundly admired. It was indeed a necessary ingredient in much of the material advancement of their societies for which communist regimes have been responsible. It seems to me, however, that it would be sociologically quite extraordinary if such asceticism were widely shared among the mass of poor peasants and workers, though it may be shared by a small and atypical minority of them. Nor can I find this morally reprehensible. I hold that extreme material poverty is so painful (literally and metaphorically) and so intellectually and emotionally stunting and narrowing (for those who are poor by circumstances and not by choice) that the desire to get 'up and out' any way, at any price, seems to me not only normal but healthy. It is, however – and this is the important point – an attitude which is more or less incompatible with the creation and maintenance of a meaningfully socialist society. This is one of the prime reasons why I hold that truly socialist societies can only be created when the material conditions which make such a desperate, clambering individualism necessary have been abolished.

So in short, I hold that materially poor societies cannot produce the democratic public life which is an essential prerequisite of the creation of socialist democracies, because gross material poverty and isolation as well as the illiteracy and narrowed intellectual vision which accompanies these material conditions make the majority of their citizens inactive or ineffective as continuous monitors and controllers of the use of public power. This means that even where that power is supposedly exercised in their interests (in Third World socialist societies), the majority is not effective in shaping definitions of what this 'general interest' is. Rather, these definitions are entirely in the hands of a ruling party or group. In many other Third World societies, of course, there is no pretence (let alone the actuality) that power is exercised in the general interest. Moreover, in both underdeveloped capitalist and socialist states in the Third World there is a more or less open self-interest operative in public life and especially in the exercise of public office. This problem is most pronounced in peripheral capitalist states (especially in Africa) where the covering for this self-interest is a thin and cynical rhetoric. In Third World socialist societies a real ideological motivation may exist among a top party élite, but at lower levels this often also gives way to a more or less opportunistic manipulation of rhetoric by a mass of middle and lower level cadres 'on the make' (usually drawn from the ranks of the peasantry and working class). In short, and to revert to the traditional analogy, in poor capitalist and socialist societies the material 'base' determines 'the superstructure' of politics in a relatively direct and crude way, at least in this one, vital respect.

However, if the hypothesis advanced at the beginning of this book is correct, then the process of industrialization and economic development in the Third World could lead to the gradual weakening of both these tendencies. In particular, if industrialization and a general and massive rise in material living standards in the Third World can occur either through capitalism or socialism (and this of course is a highly contentious issue which I shall not discuss here, though I have dealt with it at greater length in my professional work), then one may see a persistent expansion in the size and class 'depth' of public life and the increased role of genuinely ideological dispute in both the exercise of and opposition to governmental power. In short, the gradual 'freeing' or release of more and more people into self-conscious and informed political activity which has occurred in industrialized societies may occur in the Third World too, and with it the intensification of class, gender and other struggles.

In assessing the relative merits of the various types of economy and society in the Third World it seems clear that one would, from this perspective, support any political and economic system which can deliver such a transition (a) as quickly as possible and (b) at the least possible social and human cost. The problem here, of course, as is all too well and painfully known, is that criterion (a) above may be somewhat at odds with criterion (b). One therefore comes to the commonplace but necessarily elastic formulation that one would want as much of (a) as is compatible with (b). It is the experience of China above all, but also that of North Korea, which maintains my conviction that some socialist form of dictatorship presents the best prospect of a rapid transition on these terms, and to that degree I remain an old-fashioned 'Third Worldist' Marxist. But I must also say that the evidence on this is by no means unambiguous, and indeed there may be no simple generalization that one can make on the matter.

Certainly a comparison of the socialist with the capitalist road in Africa using the above criteria does not by any means show the 'capitalist road' states in the worst light.

If such industrial transitions can succeed (whether under capitalism or socialism), then at least the necessary condition of the creation of a democratic public life (the freeing of the majority of the citizens of such countries from the constrictions of absolute poverty) will be satisfied. But since, to repeat once again, this is not a sufficient condition for the creation of such a public life (and the possibility of a transition to socialist democracy which it provides), there can be no guarantee that such a public life will emerge. In fact, determined struggle to create and expand political consciousness and activity to wider and wider groups of the population of the Third World must be, and to a degree already is, a prime goal of socialists and radicals in such societies.

Where political dictatorship coexists with, and sustains, a massive maldistribution of *already abundant* wealth (as, for example, in South Africa or Brazil), then the objectives of revolutionary struggle, at least in broad terms, are clear enough. The situation is altogether more problematic, however, for socialists living in peripheral capitalist societies which are still themselves absolutely poor (i.e. where even a very radical redistribution of existing wealth would not lift general living standards to any great extent). A very good example of these problems is the situation in Kenya, a Third World society with which I am personally familiar. Until comparatively recently, socialists and radicals in Kenya believed they had a concrete alternative 'model' for development applicable to Kenya in the experience of their socialist neighbour, Tanzania. Very recently, however, abundant evidence has begun to emerge that there has been an absolute fall in the standards of living of a large part, if not a majority, of Tanzania's poor peasants and workers since the late 1960s. Faced with such evidence, some radical Kenyans have moved to embrace a more cautiously 'reformist' position vis-à-vis Kenyan capitalism, seeking to spread the benefits of economic growth there more widely whilst maintaining the basic mechanisms for capital accumulation and growth. It is easy to dismiss such shifts as capitulations to opportunism and reformism, but they do represent one response (admittedly not the only possible one) to the erosion of old certainties.

Radicals and socialists in Kenya will no doubt grope their way forward, dealing with this problem and others and arguing about them as they move from one situation to the next. It can certainly not be the role of a British academic at his typewriter to dictate what those responses should or could be, nor would this even be possible. The point of this discussion is rather to observe that an evolutionist perspective on socialist construction does not entail, in the Third World any more than in the west, that socialists should simply sit around as passive observers of capitalism, until the forces of production and material and social conditions have 'ripened' sufficiently for socialism to be on some historical 'agenda'. On the contrary, under certain conditions, even in comparatively poor societies, the growth of material prosperity and the struggle to create a politically conscious citizenry and a democratic public life can proceed hand in hand, albeit uneasily.

But such a symbiotic process of political and economic transformation (each facilitating the other) emerges a lot more easily in poor societies with a degree of formal political freedom (of speech, of assembly, of political representation) than in a poor socialist or capitalist dictatorship. Under the latter types of system the contradiction between the creation of an ever more materially prosperous and politically aware citizenry and working class and the monopoly of political and economic power by small élites is likely eventually to explode in popular demands for democratic reform and (under capitalism especially) for the redistribution of income and wealth. Paradoxically, in the transformation of socialist dictatorships into socialist democracies the working class is likely to concentrate on specifically political and constitutional demands in a narrow sense – that is on demands, at least initially, for 'bourgeois' freedoms (of speech, of assembly, of the press and media, of political representation) which have been explicitly denied in the pursuit of industrialization. In revolution against capitalist dictatorships such demands will also be made, but in addition a social and economic programme (for the redistribution of income and wealth) will have equal prominence. The current struggle in Poland exemplifies the first case, and those in South Africa and Brazil the second.

However, where the exercise of political power and the conduct of political debate has been monopolized by small minorities (whether under capitalism or socialism), the majority, even as their material standard of living rises, as educational standards improve, and as an ideological consciousness of oppression and the possibility of freedom emerges, may nurture strongly utopian or millennial expectations of what 'the revolution' can bring. Such expectations occur precisely because the desire for freedom has not been disciplined by the possibility of open debate or (even more importantly) by the exercise of political power and responsibility. Such inflated and vague expectations can lead to massive problems in the post-revolutionary situation, even if, to a degree, they are a prerequisite of a people finding the courage and hope to make a revolution in the first place. The recent tragic events in Iran are perhaps a perfect example of this phenomenon.

Reflections

If we ask why public life is the way it is in so many Third World societies, one factor strikes us immediately. In situations in which the majority of people (or even perhaps a sizeable minority) are absolutely poor, in which most people are still struggling to obtain or retain some freedom from the constraints of really basic want and deprivation, life is much more of a scrambling struggle for survival than in richer societies. The situation is reminiscent of what the modern 'game' theorists of politics call a 'zero/sum' game (i.e. a game with absolute winners and total losers) and what Thomas Hobbes, the great seventeenth-century English political theorist, called a 'war of all against all'. In such a situation where societies are emerging from absolute material poverty, people are much more prone to regard all their activities, all their investments of time and energy, from the point of view of their material 'pay off'. Thus, the pursuit of public office is simply one of many different strategies which may be followed to the same end – the escape from poverty and the pursuit of affluence. Precisely how and why the peoples of the Third World, and particularly the dominant groups in such societies, came to acquire these material aspirations and goals – the role of western influences in creating such aspirations – is a question which I cannot go into here, though it is certainly significant. The central point is simply that this kind of desperate scrambling individualism is so pronounced in poor societies, precisely because not only do winners take all, but losers lose out absolutely. The cost of failing to take advantage of opportunities for enrichment and indeed the cost of not having access to such opportunities can be an absolute poverty: a stark, constraining and total deprivation. Thus, the stakes tend to be much higher in political conflicts: the room for manoeuvre more limited, the penalties for defeat more onerous and the rewards for victory more prized.

Such a situation is to be contrasted with that in more materially prosperous societies where, since absolute poverty and deprivation is much less in evidence, political conflicts over the resources in society are much less of a 'zero/sum' game, i.e. losers rarely lose absolutely, and the privileges of the victorious in political conflicts, though considerable, are not to be contrasted with the total deprivation of the losers. This situation, of greater 'play' or room for manoeuvre is what allows, in my view, for a certain relative autonomy of political dispute and conflict from crude material self-interest. To be more precise, this relative autonomy resides in the way that both individual and group interests in prosperous capitalist democracies have to be presented if they are to be regarded as politically legitimate. It is accepted, of course, that politics and political dispute is, in large part, about conflicts of interest among individuals and groups in society. But precisely because some way has to be found of adjudicating among such interests, an essential part of the rules of the democratic game is that individuals and groups must argue that what is in their interest is also in 'the general interest'. The form that this 'general interest' takes can vary. Some individuals and groups may make demands and justify their actions in terms of the 'national interest' or of regional interests, or of the interests of a class, a racial group, a gender, an occupational group or even 'society as a whole' (there is obviously often a considerable overlap between this and the claimed 'national interest'). Often, claims are made that the interests of a particular group ('the proletariat', 'the City', 'moderate opinion', 'women') reflect the 'true' general interest, and on the other hand, counter claims may be made that the pursuit or satisfaction of these particular interests or demands would be damaging to the 'true' general interest. But precisely because in advanced capitalist democracies any particular definition of the general interest can be challenged by a competing definition, individuals and groups are aware that simply asserting that a particular sectional interest is co-extensive with the general interest ('what is good for General Motors is good for America') will not do. It is incumbent upon every competing interest group to provide a definition of what the general interest is and to show precisely why, for example, what is good for GM is good for America.

Socialists are no exception here. They may decry, and rightly, the attempt to pass off the interests of the bourgeoisie as the interests of 'the nation as a whole', but did not Marx himself argue that the overthrow of capitalism and the creation of socialism would be a liberation for the capitalists as well as for the workers? Did he not indeed say that the role of the working class under socialism would be to liquidate itself as a separate class by becoming extensive with the whole of 'civil society'? (See Chapter 5 below for what this might mean in practice.)

I believe that this 'relative autonomy' of political debate and conflict from particular sectional interests is only possible because groups and individuals who lose out in political conflicts in prosperous societies do not lose out absolutely. Hence, if their definition of the general interest is not accepted or is defeated by another they will live (usually in moderate comfort) to fight another day. In other words, it is the general prosperity underlying advanced capitalist politics which allows these 'rules of the game' (centred around competing concepts of the general interest) to be observed. To put the matter cynically, people are prepared to believe in these rules of public debate and conflict (and most people do genuinely believe in them) and to abide by their outcomes (albeit with grumbles) because they can afford to abide by them and they don't suffer too much in doing so.

Similarly, those holding public office in advanced capitalist societies do not (generally) use such office for private gain and do endeavour to pursue the general interest as they perceive it (although of course those perceptions will contain significant biases). But again, generally they are enabled to make this distinction between their public roles and their private economic interests precisely because they can afford to do so. Not only do they themselves enjoy a moderately privileged material life, but very often they are born into social classes which have enjoyed such privileges over many generations

Thus, although both individual material interests and the interests of particular groups and classes are still the essential forces at play in the politics of advanced capitalist societies, the form in which those interests are publicly expressed and argued over allows for a real 'distance' to open up between political and public debate and those interests. This 'distance' or 'relative autonomy' of politics from economics and class interests rests, however, on the general material prosperity of these societies. Conversely, when societies are very poor, there is much less space, much less room for manoeuvre to allow that distance to open up. Thus political and public life resembles much more closely a violent scramble for spoils (sometimes open, sometimes, as in many Third World socialist societies, hidden), and political life is much more comprised of a thin and cynical rhetoric, used in a more or less open fashion as an instrument of individual and group enrichment.

So what one is suggesting here is that the extent to which politics is simply a 'reflection' of economic interests and the extent to which it obtains an autonomy from the former is something which is historically variable both between societies and within one society through time. My own view, for example, is that this autonomy has increased markedly, over the long term, only in those societies which have experienced a long and sustained process of industrialization and economic growth. For it is only in such societies that significant numbers of people have been released from the imperatives of poverty and of escape from poverty (and not only in one generation but through several generations). They are thus able to think and act in the public realm with concepts of the general interest which subsume, but go beyond, their own individual self-interest or class interests. It is very clear, for example, that the relative autonomy of politics from very narrowly conceived self-interest was very much less in seventeeth or eighteenth century England than it is now.

What this suggests then is the somewhat paradoxical generalization that the more materially prosperous a society is, the less likely are its politics to be a simple 'reflection' of either individual or group material interests. One is therefore less likely to be able to reduce its political and ideological conflicts to such simple economic determinants. However, it is precisely because this dynamic and shifting relationship between economics and politics is one of the prime characteristics of long-term capitalist development that the essentially static debates about 'base and superstructure' in much modern Marxist theory are so fundamentally misconceived (see Appendix to this book). It is also – and this is the really important political point – why long-term capitalist development tends constantly to enlarge the opportunities for socialist politics and socialist construction, especially when it is combined with parliamentary democracy.

For, to be a socialist is not to support the working class's economic interests against those of the capitalist class. It is to believe in a particular conception of the general interest – a conception which involves transcending class self-interest through abolishing classes themselves. Thus, the less pressing the questions of sheer economic survival and increasing material consumption to the working class, the more that class can involve itself (on political and ethical grounds and not simply out of economic self-interest) in a debate about the 'real' general interest. In this debate, of course, the socialist conception is one contender. Parliamentary democracy provides an opportunity and a forum for that debate to take place.

3 / *Romantic anti-capitalism*

The previous two chapters have argued that only a socialism created out of materially prosperous capitalist societies – societies which possess an important if limited degree of real democracy and freedom – can hope to be a genuinely democratic socialism, a socialism which also enhances human freedom.

I am obsessed by the question of how that can be done, how socialism can be combined with freedom, for the simple reason that all the avowedly socialist societies actually existing in the world, and certainly all the societies self-advertised as 'Marxist', are dictatorships of one sort or another. Moreover, it can and has been argued that this is no accident. Real socialist societies, it is said, are not dictatorships simply because of the adverse historical circumstances in which they were created or because of 'flaws' or 'distortions' in the ways in which the socialist idea has been implemented. They are dictatorships, indeed totalitarian dictatorships, because in practice it is not possible to implement socialist ideals without resort to dictatorial control. Moreover, some have believed that the seeds of that totalitarianism can be seen in the ideas of Marx and Engels themselves, that their thought contains the elements which ultimately provided ground and justification for totalitarianism.

Perhaps the best known and certainly the most virulent attack of this sort upon Marxism was made by Professor Karl Popper in his book, *The Open Society and its Enemies*. There he suggests that Marx and Engels were historical 'determinists'. He sees the founders of Marxism as claiming to know the direction in which history was moving, and indeed as claiming to know the economic forces which drove history in these inevitable directions. Hence, says Popper, Marxists who believe in this 'economically determinist' theory see opponents as not merely wrong, but in a quite precise sense as 'reactionary', i.e. as trying to hold back inevitable historical progress. Moreover, they see themselves as the agents of that progress. Joseph Stalin could therefore send millions of 'reactionaries' to their death and to labour camps, secure in the knowledge that he was simply the agent of history, simply the hastener of that which was in any case inevitable.

This kind of criticism of Marxism as economically or historically 'determinist' did not originate with Popper, though he perhaps gave it its most polemical and best-known expression. But in any case, it is an allegation and a problem which socialist intellectuals have had to confront continually. Moreover, it is an allegation which has been echoed even by people who are, in other respects, quite sympathetic to socialism and Marxism. It has most recently and powerfully been expressed by E.P. Thompson in his book, *The Poverty of Theory*,* though he presents it in a much more subtle and much less polemical form than Popper.

In essence, Thompson argues that Marx was guilty of what he calls 'economism', of seeing societies as progressing through development of their economic 'forces of production'. In conceiv-

---

* E.P. Thompson, *The Poverty of Theory and other Essays*, London, Merlin Press, 1978.

ing societies in this way, Marx was, according to Thompson, guilty of propounding an overly narrow and misleading view of society and history.

In particular, Marx accepted far too readily that capitalist industrialization marked a 'progressive' change in human history. For although Karl Marx is thought of as the arch-critic of capitalism and the theorist of working class revolution, in fact he thought capitalism 'progressive', both because it massively increased the material productivity and wealth of society and because it created a working class possessed of both the need to create a socialist revolution and of the skills to run a socialist society. This indeed was the great ironic paradox of capitalist industrialization for Marx. In creating a working class, it also created the means of its own destruction and supersession. In line with this view, although Marx described in great detail the sufferings and exploitation of the first industrial and factory workers in nineteenth-century Britain, he never once doubted that the life of the new working class, for all its miseries, was an advance on the conditions of life of the bulk of people, on the 'idiocy of rural life' of the pre-industrial period.

It is this latter view, however, about which Thompson has the most severe doubts. In his own historical work, and especially in his great book, *The Making of the English Working Class*, he has cast empirical doubt upon it. In *The Poverty of Theory* he makes it clear that he thinks Marx could only have held to it because his interest in the working class was so narrow and peculiar. In a nutshell, Thompson thinks that Marx was interested in the *economic* role of industrial workers as producers of 'surplus value' and in their potential *political* role as revolutionaries, but that his interest in them did not extend much beyond that. Had it done so, Thompson believes, had it embraced the way in which these workers thought and felt, as *people*, had it considered their family and personal lives, their aspirations and beliefs, and indeed had it embraced a much broader understanding of the lives of pre-industrial peasants and artisans, then, Thompson thinks, Marx would have been much less certain of the 'progressiveness' of capitalist industrialization. And in fact in *The Making of the English Working Class*, Thompson does try to write this much broader, more humanistic history of the first industrial working class in the world, and he does indeed conclude that for most of them, capitalist industrialization was not *experienced* as in any way a 'progressive' change. On the contrary, for most of the people involved it was experienced as an almost unmitigated disaster.

Indeed for Thompson, both conventional Marxism and more traditional non-Marxist economic history share the same fault in this respect. They both think that questions about the standard of living of working people or about the advantages of industrialization over a pre-industrial world can be answered by purely economic evidence – on output, investment, *per capita* income, etc. But for Thompson there is a lot more to the notion of a 'standard of living' than mere money income, or indeed than mere material conditions (like housing, sanitation and health). It is just as important to consider the quality of life, and above all to consider the degree of freedom and unfreedom which people experience in the movement from a pre-industrial to an industrial world, the 'unmeasurable' losses in autonomy and self-determination which may nonetheless be experienced as a profound deprivation.

Not only did *The Making of the English Working Class* inspire a whole tradition of radical 'social' history with much the same humanistic outlook as its own, but for Thompson this issue of the narrowness and economism of much traditional Marxism is intimately connected to the crimes which have been committed in its name. For if one holds that no real human freedom can come about except through the material prosperity brought by industrialization, one can also come to believe that the end justifies the means, i.e. that in order to industrialize as quickly as possible and thus hasten the future realm of freedom, one is justified in denying all freedom in the present – one is justified in forced collectivization, labour camps and terror – in short, the whole Stalinist experience.

Nor does Thompson think that this is the only link between Stalinism and Marx's own thought. In Stalinist Russia, and indeed in most communist countries to this day, a rigid censorship is maintained over all cultural, artistic activity and expression. This is justified by a 'class' interpretation of cultural life, so that art, literature, music, etc., are either 'proletarian' or 'bourgeois', and state power must be used to ensure that only the former finds expression. At its most extreme this even affected the practice of natural science in the Soviet Union, whose results were doctored to fit the party line.

In *The Poverty of Theory* Thompson sees Marx as having to take some share of responsibility for this too. Marx and Engels were themselves highly cultured men who thrived on free debate and made no attempt to censor others, even when they disagreed violently with them. But nonetheless, they were, Thompson argues, prone to 'reduce' social and cultural life as a whole to economic and class issues, and therefore some of their writings do provide apparent justification for ideas of 'proletarian' art or science and the repression and censorship which has been practised in their name. The question of whether this 'economism' and 'reductionism' is a serious philosophical or theoretical problem in Marxism is a complex one, which is discussed at length in the appendix to this book. Readers who are interested in these more abstruse theoretical issues may wish to follow them there.

Here, I want simply to repeat that the desire to avoid 'economism' and 'reductionism' produces, in Thompson especially, a kind of history which is strongly social and humanistic in outlook, and which has influenced a whole tradition of radical social history which has tried to follow his example. Inspired by Thompson's *Making* . . ., a whole style of history, organized around the Ruskin History Workshop and then the *History Workshop Journal* has tried to reconstruct, in all its humanity and fullness, the history of working people in Britain (mainly but not completely from the Industrial Revolution onwards) seen in abstraction from capitalism.* That is to say, most social histories of the 'History Workshop' type have been small-scale local studies of particular groups of workers (men and women), detailed descriptions of their working conditions, family life, customs, recreations, beliefs and their political or industrial activity (strikes, sabotage, etc.). Much of it has been fascinating, and carefully and lovingly done, a realization of one of the Workshop's most important founding aims – to rescue the history of ordinary working people from the profound silence, even contempt, to which conventional economic and political history ('ruling class history') had consigned it. Capitalism appears, if at all, in this alternative 'social' history only as quickly sketched 'background conditions' (of employment in a given industry or trade, or as booms or slumps to which the particular workers have to respond) or as the enemy – employers to strike against or to resist in other ways. Indeed it is as important that this history is 'social' history as that it is 'socialist' history, i.e. it is a form of history defined against conventional economic and political history, the first concerned with macro-economic trends, and the second with the doings of 'great men' in parliament. It is a history that takes its inspiration as much from micro-sociology,

---

* Thus, for example, as Anderson points out, the detailed histories of particular groups of workers found in The Making . . . appear without any discussion of the overall occupational composition of the English working class in the period with which the book is concerned (1790–1830). When such an analysis is done we find that the groups featured in the book were in fact highly atypical of the class as a whole. As Anderson remarks, there is an 'absence from The Making of the English Working Class of any real treatment of the whole historical process whereby heterogeneous groups of artisans, smallholders, agricultural labourers, domestic workers and casual poor were gradually assembled, distributed and reduced to the condition of labour subsumed to capital', hence, 'In the absence of any objective framework laying down the overall pattern of capital accumulation in these years, there is little way of assessing the relative importance of one area of subjective experience within the English working class against another. Proportions are wanting. Selectivity of focus is combined with sweep of conclusion, typically with such passion and skill that the former can easily be forgotten by the reader' (Perry Anderson, Arguments within English Marxism, London, Verso, 1980, pp. 33 and 35).

and above all social anthropology, as from conventional history. Where conventional economic and political history operate on a national or even on an international scale, social history prefers the small-scale and intimate. Where they are concerned mainly with aggregated magnitudes and trends, it is concerned with the disaggregated and local. Where they deal with public life, social history is as much or more concerned with the 'private' realm, with the family, child-rearing, sexual relationships and recreation.

This kind of historical method (local, small-scale studies, focused on small groups of workers or individuals, and concerned with short time-spans) is essentially forced on anyone whose main aim is to 'reconstruct' the 'fullness' and 'humanity' of working-class life. But it is also, by the same token, a method which finds it hard to grasp broader-scale movements or long-term trends, and for that reason, a method which risks not seeing the macro-long-term wood for the micro-short-term trees. Thus, for example, a study designed to show the damaging effect on a community of growing local unemployment or other economic problems might mislead by omission, in that the effects of moving elsewhere to find work on both those who moved and those who were left behind are not recorded. An example may help to make this clearer. The following is an extract from a description of the enclosure of land in the Forest of Knaresborough in the late eighteenth century:

> the poor cottager and his family exchanged their indolence for active industry, and obtained extravagant wages; and hundreds were induced to offer their labour from distant quarters; labourers of every denomination, carpenters, joiners, smiths and masons poured in, and met with constant employment. And though before the allotments were set out, several riots had happened, the scene was now quite changed; for with all the foreign assistance, labour kept extravagantly high. . . . In consequence, the product is increased beyond conception,

the rent more than trebled and population advanced in a very high degree.*

Now imagine a history of enclosure in this area which started with a detailed and loving picture of the 'poor cottagers' before the enclosures, which recorded powerfully their fears and anxieties expressed as the enclosure movement commenced, and terminated with them rioting and with the forcible suppression of the riots by the local authorities. Such a history would in no way be 'untrue'. It might indeed capture a fleeting historical moment powerfully and movingly, but it would none the less be severely misleading if it failed to record that as a matter of fact, and for reasons which neither reflect credit upon others nor ill upon the cottagers, their worst forebodings were not realized. This, I think, is what a great deal of romantic anti-capitalist social history actually does. It says in effect 'their forebodings were there. They are and were as much a historical fact as the subsequent events and no less terrifying for those who experienced them because they happened, in this case, not to be justified. Only those with hindsight are spared the fear of the unknown'. This is what the privilege of 'experience' actually implies as a historical method. And in Thompson, at any rate, this kind of method was a reaction not only against the 'economistic' Marxism which he had learnt in the Communist Party (which he left in 1956 after the Soviet invasion of Hungary) but also against all of the conventional 'economic' histories of the Industrial Revolution which had been dominant when he started work on *The Making* . . . . For such histories had been 'full of capitalism' if by that is meant statistics of aggregate output, investment and of *per capita* income. All these upward sloping graphs were, together with tales of the great British entrepreneurs, the principal support for the orthodox interpre-

* G.B. Rennie, *General View of the Agriculture of the West Riding of Yorkshire*, 1794, p. 76, quoted in Harold Perkin, *The Origins of Modern English Society 1780–1880*, London, Routledge & Kegan Paul, 1969, p. 127.

tation of the British Industrial Revolution. This interpretation, then as now, sees the revolution as the most important and progressive economic transition in the history of mankind. It is seen as such because it held out for the first time the possibility (later the actuality) of ending the most gross forms of material want among the majority of people in certain societies, and perhaps (at some time) in the world as a whole. As we have already noted, Thompson wanted to mount a challenge to this whole 'progressive' interpretation of the Industrial Revolution in *The Making* . . . . But he does so by essentially describing and analysing the attitudes, beliefs, changing living patterns and political mobilization of 'working-class' people in early nineteenth-century England in abstraction from the broader macro-economic trends in the period and their social concomitants. Thus was the 'social' history of the 'working class' in Britain separated from the 'economic' history of capitalism in Britain, a separation which has become almost total in the subsequent work of the History Workshop.

But why does this matter? What is the importance of these obscure intellectual trends among a few left-wing historians? It is important because it is here that an intellectual tendency both reflects and reinforces much more widespread political attitudes and beliefs on the Left of Britain. For radical social history of the 'History Workshop' variety shares in common with large sections of the trade union leadership in this country, and with most of the people who make up the Bennite Left in the Labour Party, an attitude which I will call *romantic anti-capitalism*. This attitude sees the development of capitalism in Britain as having had only or predominantly negative and damaging consequences for working people and tends to view as heroic the struggles of any groups of workers (particularly those in threatened or marginalized occupations) against such consequences. This is the central core of its romanticism, which is also expressed in the belief that any and all aspects of the social and cultural life of 'working class' people are worthy of study, simply because they are "working class" people, or more exactly, simply because they are people, fully equal in their humanity and worth to the middle and upper classes whose history has been much more lavishly recorded (both by themselves and by more conventional historians).

However, I also characterize this attitude as anti-capitalist rather than as socialist, precisely because it is an essentially negative posture and attitude. 'History Workshop' historians, like many of the trade unionists whose history they write, and like many Labour Party activists to whose ranks they frequently belong, know what they are against but are much less clear what they are for. They are essentially resisters, rather than revolutionaries, because though they lament and attack capitalism's impact upon the lives of working people past and present, they really have very few ideas, or indeed no ideas at all, about how, and in what precise respects, capitalism can be changed.

For once one turns one's attention to this issue, and indeed to the experience of the socialist societies which actually exist in the world, one question immediately strikes home. It is this. Which of the constraints which capitalism imposes upon working people would be common to any form of complex industrial economy, and which are unique to capitalism itself? The former would clearly be unalterable by a change to socialism, the latter would not be. Therefore, one must have this distinction clear in order to create any realistic socialist strategy. However, as soon as one tries to draw these distinctions clearly, complex issues of economic theory and organization are immediately raised. I have tried to deal with some of them in Chapter 1 (pp. 41–3). But it is not possible to raise them, let alone resolve them, unless some economic issues are confronted. And it is a mark of radical social history, as indeed it is a mark of the British Labour Party past and present, that it is notoriously weak on economics. Indeed, it can be said of the latter, as of the former, that effectively it has no economic theory.

And if one asks for the Labour Party, and indeed for British socialism in general, why this is, the answer is not far to seek. It lies in the formation of the Labour Party, and indeed of most of the nineteenth-century socialist groups in Britain, in an intellectual ambiance which was distanced from classical political economy (indeed most of the earliest socialist thinkers in Britain defined their ideas against Adam Smith and the classical school), from its neo-classical successor and from Marxist economics. Hostile to all of these economic creeds (again mainly on humanistic grounds) British socialism, and especially the Labour Party, has been dominated by intellectuals, such as the Fabians, who are strong on social policy but weak on economics. Or to put the matter more accurately, it was and is dominated by people who are concerned overwhelmingly with how income and wealth, once created, can be more equitably distributed and put to 'welfarist' uses, but who are much less interested in the process of wealth production itself. And it is interesting that when the Labour Party did find its 'own' economic theorist, or rather when, after the war, it adopted *in toto* the economic theory of John Maynard Keynes, it was adopting the theory of a man who was a Liberal in politics and indeed avowedly *anti*-socialist in his fundamental attitudes and beliefs. And significantly, Keynesian economics, like Fabian social policy, rested on the assumption that the basic problem of how to produce an increasing quantity of material goods and services ('economic growth') had been solved by the capitalist market economy. The issue for Keynes was how to keep that growth proceeding steadily (rather than via booms and slumps) and how to make it compatible with the maintenance of full employment. And of course it was this essentially welfarist objective of Keynesian economics (full employment) which attracted both the Labour Party and the trade unions to it.

But why has British socialism always had such a distaste for economics and economic theory in any form, and why has it had so few economists among its intellectuals? I think principally because concentration upon the fundamental long-term mechanisms of growth and accumulation forces questions upon one which a romantic anti-capitalism cannot cope with. For example: (1) Is it or is it not true that real wages must be kept in line with increases in labour productivity in order to avoid inflation?

(2) Is it or is it not true that money wage increases won by trade unions which are not matched by increases in productivity will prove of short-lived value to the workers who gain them (i.e. that they will be eaten away by inflation)?

(3) Is it or is it not true that in any economic system savings will have to be made out of current consumption to fund investment, and that therefore the 'full product' of labour can never, under any system producing a continuous increase in material living standards, accrue to the workers who produced it?

(4) In any event, does it now make any sense to consider production or net investment as a product simply of 'labour'?

(5) If capital contributes with labour to the creation of profit (and thus to investment), does that mean that capitalists are an essential or irreplaceable part of a market economy?

(6) Is it true that a market mechanism is the most efficient means yet discovered of keeping the use of resources (land, labour, natural resources) broadly in line with the relative supply of those resources? Or at least,

(7) Is it not demonstrably more efficient than central planning has proven to date?

(8) Is it true that if economic sectors and activities are kept in being by various forms of government subsidy, the effect in the medium to long term is to lower total output in the economy, and thus to damage the welfare of those subsidized, even if it maintains or increases such welfare in the short term?

For what it is worth, my answer to these questions would be: (1) true; (2) true; (3) true; (4) it makes no sense; (5) no it does not; (6) true; (7) yes; and (8) depends on very particular circumstances, but for the moment it does not matter what the answers are. The central point is simply that these are the sort of questions one must be able to answer if one is to be serious about attempting to create an alternative to capitalism, and indeed in determining what precise kind of alternative is feasible. They are also, one may say, the kind of questions one must be able to answer if one is to have any effective reply to monetarism. However – and this is the point – one does not have to have an answer if one is simply concerned with resistance to what is, rather than with the creation of an alternative. Indeed, if one is simply concerned with resistance, it is better not even to ask these types of questions for fear that asking them might weaken morale among the resisters.

And this is the central point really: 'History Workshop' history, as the history of resistance, is the perfect intellectual counterpart to traditional British trade unionism, which is also, and above all, a movement of resistance. And the essential requirement of resistance to capitalism, within capitalism, is that one must have a morality, an ethic, upon which resistance is based. Thus the essential question is not 'Is capitalism efficient?' (this is a question only for capitalists) but 'Is it fair?' The question is not 'Did (Do) capitalists accumulate?' but 'Did (Do) they treat their workers well?' The essential question is not 'What determines the distribution of income and wealth under capitalism?' but 'Is such a distribution fair or just or right?'

Now certainly such an ethic or morality is both necessary and desirable for socialists because it helps them to ask some of the right political questions. How can the distribution of income and wealth be made fairer? How can production and economic enterprise in general be carried on in ways which allow all those people involved to treat each other better? But such questions are also potentially dangerous, because if left in this pure ethical form they are seriously incomplete and misleading. For the altogether tougher questions are, for example, 'How can the distribution of income and wealth be made fairer at the same time as maintaining an at least minimally efficient form of wealth creation?' Or, 'How can economic enterprises and other organizations be made more democratic whilst maintaining sufficient discipline to ensure that their essential functioning is not impaired?' These and questions like them are the really tough questions for socialism to answer both in theory and practice. They are what might be termed *ethico-technical* questions, and one cannot come to terms with them through a socialist morality alone. They also involve the use of both economic and political theory. And to repeat, without such theory, what one has is simply an ethic of resistance within capitalism (romantic anti-capitalism). It is an ethic which simply sells the pass, by leaving it up to the intellectual apologists for capitalism (conventional economists usually) to treat the hard economic issues on their terms. Romantic anti-capitalism is thus also the perfect intellectual equivalent of the practical trade union attitude of 'leaving it to the managers to manage' (see the final chapter of this book). It buys a kind of moral purity at the cost of an ultimate soft-headedness, a soft-headedness from which only the apologists for capitalism, and indeed capitalism itself, can benefit.

Above all, romantic and anti-capitalism makes it almost impossible to come to terms with the present political implications of what I conceive of as the true historical picture of capitalist development in Britain and indeed elsewhere – this damnably difficult dialectic of real but limited freedom and democracy, of potentialities created but simultaneously frustrated, of co-existant organization and anarchy – with which I tried to grapple in the previous two chapters and to which I return again and again throughout this book. In its mistaken belief that 'economism' leads either to a capitulation to capitalist rationality or to Stalinism, romantic anti-capitalism prevents socialists in Britain from having a realistic view of the past, and more importantly prevents a clear-headed engagement with the problems of socialist construction in the present. By its refusal to acknowledge whole-heartedly (rather than reluctantly) the real material benefits which the bulk of the people both in Britain and in the western world in general have obtained from capitalist development and the changes in their attitudes which this prosperity has brought, romantic anti-capitalism (the thinking of the Bennite Left in the Labour Party is a prime example) also generates a politics which has virtually no popular resonance and which is bound therefore to remain a ghetto politics.

4 / Feminism: potential and actuality

The growth of a socialist feminist movement (as part of a general rebirth of feminism) not only in Britain but all over the western world is one of the most important new social and political phenomena of the post-war period. As part of a generalized critique of male dominated politics, socialist feminists pointed out that traditional Left movements and parties had operated with perfectly conventional gender hierarchies (men in power, women in generally subordinate roles). They also emphasized that the dominant focus of traditional Left activity – the 'working class' – had in fact usually been interpreted as 'male manual workers' in blatant disregard of the actual sexual composition of the wage labour force in Britain and elsewhere, and in implicit reinforcement of the conventional non-radical view that the political views and opinions of women could be 'subsumed' in that of 'their' men (husbands, fathers, brothers, etc.).

Starting from such simple but powerful and significant truths, the feminist movement has subsequently extended its critique, analysis and political activity into virtually every area of Left activity. It has made influential critiques of radical and socialist history, of the structure and organization of traditional Left parties and radical movements, and indeed of a whole range of ideologies and social and economic institutions in capitalist and socialist societies. In all these cases feminists have been preoccupied with the complex relationships between class exploitation and gender exploitation, and in particular with the question of the autonomy of the latter, its irreducibility to the former, and the sorts of separate or autonomous struggle that are necessary to overcome it. In the course of such analyses socialist feminists have done new and important intellectual work on the 'hidden' history of feminism and of women in general and on the structure and role of the family in western capitalism. They have been particularly concerned with the role of the family in creating and maintaining public and private gender roles and stereotypes. As a result of this veritable explosion of intellectual and political activity by women on the Left, the whole radical movement has been profoundly and irreversibly transformed. It is now impossible for anyone who wishes to be called a socialist to be unconcerned with issues of sexual dominance and repression, with the particular forms of repression that women suffer in our society, and with the new dimensions that such understandings inevitably impose on our conception of what a genuinely socialist future would involve. There is no doubt, too, that for many male socialists this feminist critique has been a personally painful one to confront, requiring as it does attempts to change both attitudes and behaviour which previously it had been possible to relegate to a separate sphere of 'private life' to which 'political' principles were 'not relevant'.

It is important to say all this, because most of the rest of this chapter will be rather critical in tone, and it might therefore appear to be anti-feminist or to be calling into question the fundamental feminist critique and restatement of socialist theory and practice in Britain. It intends neither. On the contrary, most of what appears below could not have been written without that critique. Its fundamental point is that in its beginnings feminism made a devastatingly powerful criticism of much of the interpersonal style and form of male-dominated Left activity and seemed to promise an alternative which might have helped the Left clamber out of the ghetto mentality of which that style was both a symptom and a reinforcement. I will argue, however, that in practice feminism, or rather many feminists, have not followed through that criticism into their own practice. In fact they have sadly reproduced much of that style in their own activity, with gravely damaging consequences for feminism, for the responses of both women and men to that feminism, and for the socialist and radical movement in general. Indeed, I argue below that feminism itself is now largely a ghetto, marked by much the same kind of self-insulating behaviour which has traditionally marked some more orthodox Left sects.

We should start, therefore, with the original feminist critique of the Left. Several early feminist studies of the socialist and radical movements in Britain pointed out that Left movements (and especially the conventional Left sects) had traditionally operated with an almost total insensitivity to the interpersonal dimension of what they were doing. From the perspective of almost every sect, other human beings were always seen *instrumentally*, as 'workers' or 'students' to be recruited, as the bearers of 'false consciousness' to be 'demystified', as 'liberals' to be 'won over' or 'neutralized', or as opponents or reactionaries to be 'crushed'. This instrumental attitude meant, in turn that only such characteristics of outsiders that were of relevance (positively or negatively) to the sect or party were of interest to it. Hence potential recruits were always scrutinized for signs of 'confusion', 'contradiction' or vestiges of 'liberal delusions'. Indeed, the only attitudes or beliefs of liberals that were of interest were those which might be of use in their being won over or neutralized. This essential instrumentality, argued feminists, sprang directly from the nature of Left sects and parties which defined themselves as already in possession of the truth (or rather of 'correct' positions) on a vast range of issues. Thus people outside, even potential recruits, had nothing to offer to such parties, and plumbing the depths of their experience and consciousness, their world view, was simply a waste of time. 'Does X support the party's position, or is he/she recruitable or definable with reference to some aspect of it ?': these were the only relevant questions. This ideologically determined instrumentality and insensitivity in personal relations (at least between sect or party members and others) also produced a view of argument as a battle to be won. As a party militant, one did not enter into a debate or argument with an outsider or political opponent in order to learn anything oneself. One entered into it in order to convert the opponent, or at least to demonstrate the 'correctness' of one's own (i.e. the party's) position. Feminists saw this highly aggressive style of argument with its frequent use of analogies drawn from battle or warfare as derived from the male domination of most Left activity, as a sort of intellectual and political *machismo*. They also saw such behaviour as not merely unpleasant and inhuman but as politically counter-productive. They argued that its net effect was actually to alienate many potential supporters and recruits by reinforcing all the stereotypes which socialism's opponents use to such effect ('dogmatic fanaticism', etc.). A prime aim of the feminist movement therefore was not merely to change the kinds of issues and questions that were debated and struggled over on the Left, but actually to change the way in which such debate was carried on and the forms of organization and decision-making within which it occurred. In particular, there was a desire to move away from the 'democratic-centralist' hierarchy which most Left sects had slavishly copied from the Bolsheviks, and to adopt much looser, more democratic forms of organization. To a considerable degree the latter objective was achieved, and the Women's Movement in Britain has been and remains very notable for its lack of hierarchy and structure and for its genuinely collective style of work. I believe, however, that this change of structure has not in fact generally been accompanied by the associated change in the style of debate, argument and interpersonal relationships in feminist activity. In particular, it seems to me two sets of relationships remain profoundly problematic for feminists. These are: (1) relationships with non-feminist women, and (2) relationships with men in general, and in particular with male 'comrades' in Left and radical movements.

I shall deal with (1) first and devote most space to it, for in the current state of development of the Women's Movement it is politically the most important problem. Perhaps the most exciting single aspect of the Women's Movement at its inception was its potential appeal to half of humanity, its promise to bring into the centre of political debate and activity a vast underclass which had previously been relegated to an entirely peripheral position within the socialist movement, and indeed within political and public life generally. In broad conformity with the M/K criterion which I outlined in Chapter 1, the feminist movement set out both to expand the range of issues to be seen as public and political and to claim for half the adult citizens of our country a place in its public life which they had been denied for centuries. Thus, any factors or behaviour which threaten the Women's Movement's actual capacity to reach and influence this vast potential constituency, which tend in fact to confine it to a tiny, sociologically distinct minority of women, must be a serious cause for concern for feminists themselves and for all who support their feminist cause. I shall argue that there are such factors at work, and that far from being unique to the feminist movement they are in fact very recognizable, indeed depressingly familiar. For these factors have long haunted virtually all socialist and radical movements.

The essential problem is the following. The central thrust of feminist ideology (as of socialist ideology) is an explanation of the situation of women which identifies them as a repressed and exploited category (albeit to various degrees and with various nuances) and which identifies men (again to various degrees) as a repressive and exploiting category. However, it is a complex but tolerably clear fact that many, perhaps even the majority of women do not see themselves as repressed and exploited, or men as repressors and exploiters. They may indeed recognize that they suffer certain forms of disability and discrimination *as women*, and may even resent these forms. But the explanation that they will offer of them will not necessarily be that which identifies men as their oppressors, or which indeed sees solutions in feminine solidarity or identification with the Women's Movement. Such explanations can be enormously varied, from the fatalistic ('it's always been that way and it always will be') to the contingent ('I was just a bit depressed', 'he was very upset') and to the sociologically forgiving ('you can't really blame them, it's just the way they were brought up'). But whatever the forms of explanation offered, whether they acknowledge the problem but 'explain it away' or deny its existence altogether, feminists are in a position where they cannot accept these explanations as of equal validity with their own. In other words, part of what it means to say one is a feminist is that one privileges, one must privilege, 'feminist' explanations and understandings of the situation of women over the explanations and understandings of that situation offered by non-feminist women. Certainly, one can and must endeavour to explain why non-feminist women offer these sorts of explanations of their situation; one must endeavour to understand 'women's consciousness' in all its forms. And feminist literature is not short of such explanations. Indeed much feminist work on family life, on education systems and on the media is motivated by just such objectives. But when all such exercises are completed, though one may understand, one cannot share or evaluate such understandings as 'equally valid' with one's own. In the end, one must hold that such understandings are partial, confused, confining. In short, one must, as a feminist, just as a socialist, be committed to some concept of 'false consciousness'. To be a feminist among non-feminist women, just as to be a socialist worker among non-socialist workers, is necessarily to be denied the comfort or the escape of a thorough-going relativism. This is not a comfortable position, involving as it does some necessary implication that one knows better than the people who are themselves having certain experiences how to explain what they are experiencing. But comfortable or not, all socialists and radicals (including feminists) are landed with this problem. One may say, advisedly, that it is a cross we all have to bear, replete with ethical and political dangers but inescapable.

This being the case, the crucial issue becomes not how to escape it, but the implications or effect that the necessary privileging of one's own explanations over other people's will have on the way one treats such people when one meets them (in this case how feminist women treat non-feminist women when they meet them).

Before commenting on feminism in this regard, let me offer a word or two about the Left in general. My observation is that when this 'acid test' is set, most leftists and radicals fail it abysmally. For however subtle and modulated may be their explanations of the consciousness of the oppressed and of the causes of its formation and deformation, when confronted with the actual expressed attitudes and values which are most threatening to radicals and socialists, their actual face-to-face response is often either (a) retreat, or (b) contempt, or (c) violent denunciation, or (d) some combination of (a) and (b) or (b) and (c). Rarely if ever is there an attempt actually to engage rationally with such attitudes, to argue against them in a way that accords the 'reactionary' in question (note incidentally how rapidly we are driven in these situations to drop the qualifications and modulations and to define the other clearly as 'enemy') any legitimacy or indeed any identity as a thinking or feeling person.

I do not say this in any spirit of superiority. I am only too aware from personal and painful experience that the test is so often failed because it is so easy to fail. For however sophisticated and 'humanist' one's analyses and explanations of false consciousness may be in the abstract, when actually confronted with assertions that the wogs should be sent home, or that homosexuals should be castrated, or that communists are running the trade unions, any of the responses above ((a), (b) or (c)) are a lot easier than commencing a long, painful and probably fruitless argument, in which one has first to establish some relationship that would even make it possible for the 'falsely conscious' person in question to take what one says seriously.

Now the point of course is that there are perfect feminist equivalents for all this. There are women who announce aggressively how much they enjoy being a girl, who assert that all feminists are lesbians, or who denounce the vileness and wickedness of working mothers even if they are single parents. And my observation, sadly, is that placed in such situations the actual track record of feminist women is broadly similar to and certainly no better than any other group of socialists or radicals. In particular, the temptation for feminists as for other radical minorities in such situations is to retreat, to gather together with those who at least share some of one's basic values and assumptions, and there, secure in 'sisterhood', to commence or continue debate, analysis and argument. Moreover, in such a situation of retreat, one may adopt (consciously or not) modes of behaviour and patterns of dress of speech which signal one's shared identity (in this case one's feminist identity). But the adoption of this strategy just sets one further apart from other women, the majority of women, for whom 'in theory' one is struggling. And so there is a familiar and painful paradox in which feminists, like many other radicals, find themselves ensnared. They are 'radical democrats' in principle and rhetoric, reaching out to and speaking for all women. But in practice, often in order just to survive and remain intact psychologically and emotionally, they must reach for an unintended but nevertheless obvious (to outsiders) élitism and exclusiveness.

But the retreat can often take other forms too. One of particular significance is the tendency to associate predominantly or even solely with men who accept at least some feminist premises. This reflection brings us to the second problematic area for feminists identified earlier – relationships with men. Now to some extent this relationship is understandably and justifiably going to be a difficult one, simply because a feminist movement is a feminist movement. Individual feminists may or may not see men in general as 'the enemy' (though, as is well known, some radical feminists certainly do). But whether individuals have this attitude or not, structually the feminist movement as a whole – committed to the view that all societies are permeated with degrees of sexism and patriarchal power – must see men in general as involved (again to varying degrees) in the oppression of women. Necessarily, therefore, relationships with individual members of a gender defined as oppressive (even if also seen as suffering themselves some oppression in a sexist society) must create problems. At the very least it must involve a heightened consciousness of the potential difficulties and inequalities that are involved in relating to, or working with, male comrades. No man who takes the feminist critique at all seriously, or purports to acknowledge the broad truth of its position can be insensitive to these problems, or refuse to alter or monitor his own behaviour in order to minimize them. What follows is not therefore a complaint about the fact that feminists necessarily make demands upon men in general, and in particular upon male comrades. 'Solidarity' means nothing if words are not matched by deeds. Even to be seen to be struggling genuinely to overcome sexist attitudes and behaviour involves changing or trying to change very deeply rooted attitudes and behaviour. If that is not easy, it is the perfectly justified price demanded for having one's claim to 'solidarity' taken seriously.

The problem in which I see the feminist movement involved in its relationships with men is somewhat different from all this, and once again, it is a depressingly familiar one, with at least one, almost exact, predecessor. In fact it is worth taking the predecessor first, so that the essential structural problem can be revealed through it. If one is involved in radical ethnic politics, if one is a leader or militant in a movement of blacks or of Asians, one obviously does not spend much time in the company of avowed white supremacists. The reasons are obvious enough: their views and beliefs are so hostile to one's own that there is simply no basis upon which any kind of relationship could be developed. The only alternatives available are to remain apart from such people or to be involved in 'battle' with them. The probability in fact is that in a society in which the white majority is saturated with racism (albeit, and importantly, to varying degrees), one will spend little time at all in the company of whites.

One may of course have a limited functional interaction with them (in the economic marketplace primarily), but beyond that it is quite likely that one's contact with the white majority will be minimal; certainly one will have few or no friends and comrades there. Moreover, if and when one is in closer contact with whites, it is almost certain that these will be white liberals or radicals, themselves acutely aware of, opposed to, and guilty about the existence of white racism in their society.

All this leads to a totally comprehensible but rather curious result. In Britain, as indeed in the USA and elsewhere, black militants and militants from other ethnic minority groups, in so far as they associate closely (even relatively closely) with whites at all, associate with a highly atypical and guilt-ridden minority. This in turn can have two further consequences. Firstly, the mere fact of associating predominantly with such an atypical minority can lead to a gradual but real loss of perspective on the general situation. That is, one comes to concentrate predominantly or even solely on the contradictions and weaknesses, even the hidden racism, in the attitudes of 'white liberals', gradually forgetting or ignoring the fact that in comparison with the vast white majority 'out there' the liberals hardly count as racists at all. Sometimes this distortion of vision can even get to the point that the 'hypocrisies' of white liberalism are seen as worse than the 'honesty' of undisguised bigotry. 'White liberals', simply because one knows enough about them to be able to see and sense certain hypocrisies and evasions, come under ever more critical scrutiny, whilst their atypicality among whites as a whole is either denied or ignored or derided for complicating what would otherwise be a clear and 'honest' racial division.

The second consequence that can flow from the predominant association of black militants with highly defensive and guilt-ridden white liberals is that this guilt is sensed and used by the militants to exercise a certain kind of power and moral blackmail. That is, the continual fear of being denounced as 'racist' leads white liberals to support, or at least to assent to, arguments which if advanced by whites would meet counter-arguments or resistance. At the psychologically 'sick' extreme, this can even lead to situations in which blacks behave in more and more outrageous ways, or advance ever more extreme arguments just to see how far this guilt-ridden assent will stretch. For of course, highly perceptive and politically astute black militants see such white liberal assent, quite correctly, as itself racist. It is indeed this sort of behaviour that precisely generates black accusations of white liberal 'hypocrisy' and 'paternalism'. But such accusations ignore the fact that in certain situations white liberals and black militants can lock themselves into a very sick and self-generating syndrome in which black allegations and accusations (actual or feared) lead to white liberal defensiveness and ritualistic assent; this in turn leads to denunciations of 'hypocrisy' and 'paternalism', which generates further assent and ritualistic self-exculpation, producing further denunciations, and so on. The net result of course is that the honesty with others and with oneself and the mutual trust which would allow productive debate and genuine comradeship and friendship to emerge are never present or given a chance to manifest themselves. Instead, relationships between black militants and white liberals or radicals merely become a painful and deeply dishonest 'inversion' of the racism of the wider society. Radicals seeking to combat that racism politically and to escape it personally simply find it seeping through remorselessly into their own endeavours, albeit in complex and psychologically 'deep' forms.

I am writing here about feminism not racism, but the point of the above discussion must I think be obvious to the reader even before I make it. For I hold that there are disquieting signs of the reproduction of just such 'sick' syndromes, at least in the institutional relationships of feminists and male radicals, i.e. in the kinds of interactions that tend to go on within political groups or movements, and within Left academic and political conferences and congresses of various sorts. In particular there are repeated examples of male ritualistic assent to all feminist demands and arguments, some of which at least are advanced on the explicit or implicit premiss that any opposition encountered from men will be denounced as 'sexist'. This latter threat (real, implied or simply sensed) in turn leads to situations in which only other women can 'legitimately' challenge arguments advanced by other women, and even situations where only women can be legitimate spokespeople on certain subjects. There are also clear signs of that self-reproducing problem of 'tokenism' and 'hypocrisy' which I talked about above. That is, faced with a real or implied threat of being denounced as sexist, men remain silent when what they regard as dubious arguments are being advanced by feminists. Such ritualistic assent, which may not be followed through by an active support, in turn generates accusations as above, which leads to further male retreats and ritualistic assent.

But here one needs to be specific and to talk about issues. Two may be taken as particularly important: (1) the issue of 'women's history' and 'women's studies' in general, and (2) the increasing tendency for feminists to found specialist groups within Left political and intellectual movements to deal with the 'women's aspect' of virtually everything.

In the first case, having established indubitably that 'radical' history and indeed virtually all other radical intellectual activity has either ignored or marginalized the role of women in society, a debate emerges about the most desirable form of corrective to this. Should the aim be to set up a separate body of historical work or of politics, sociology, economics, anthropology devoted to women, or should the aim be to reconstruct these subjects totally, so that the previously ignored 50 per cent of humanity obtains a treatment and importance commensurate with its actual role in history and society? In some ways the latter seems a more satisfactory objective, at least in the longer term, particularly because the former approach carries with it certain dangers. Two in particular stand out. First, the theoretical object of 'women's history' may lead its practitioners to adopt principles of selection when doing history which may be seriously distorting. I am thinking here of a tendency to turn women's history into a game of 'hunt the feminist' (or proto-feminist), and a tendency to select out those aspects of the history of women

which will show them as in continual struggle against 'patriarchy' or which allow women in quite different historical
circumstances to be endowed with feminist or proto-feminist
consciousness. The point here of course is not that such history is
illegitimate in itself but that it must be set within a general corpus
of work which attempts to grasp the complex and contradictory
totality of the situation of women (including the distinctly non-
feminist aspects of their relationships with men and with each
other), and which is concerned to attempt to reconstruct in full
the very different behaviour and consciousness of women (and
men) living in very different situations to our own. The second
danger is that 'women's history', and 'women's studies' in
general will be claimed *de jure* or become *de facto* an activity
carried out overwhelmingly or even solely by women scholars.
This seems to me to risk 'ghettoizing' women's studies within
academia (as has happened to a certain extent with Black Studies
in the United States), and paradoxically it may end by weakening
the actual presence of women in the social sciences and
humanities as a whole. More importantly, however, such a
tendency very much allows male academics and other 'off the
hook', since they can safely go on ignoring the issues they have
previously ignored, justifying this by an assertion that, in the
academic division of labour, those aspects are now taken care of
'by my female colleagues'. Finally, and to take what is a vocal but
minority trend within feminism, the sole right of women to do
women's studies can be defended by an essentialism that asserts
more or less crudely that 'you have to be a woman to understand
women', thereby excluding men from the subject on somewhat
mystical biological grounds. It is difficult not to be simply rude
and polemical about this sort of argument, especially since it
seems, in a quite precise sense, to have distinctly fascist
undertones. Suffice it to say therefore that anyone committed to
this position must logically also be committed to the position that
only men can understand men, and thus only men can write the
history, sociology, anthropology, etc., of men. Since I observe
that the few radical feminists who hold this position are some-

what reluctant to concede its impeccable corollary, I conclude that they have not fully thought out all the implications of their position.

We may now turn to the second problematic area of feminist activity, the increasing tendency for feminists to demand a separate or at least distinct presence within every political and academic event in which they are represented. Clearly in very many cases this is absolutely necessary. Distinct and sometimes even 'closed' women's organizations within political groups are often essential, both to discuss the specific role and position of women within the organization and, above all, to build a sense of sisterhood and consciousness among women who might otherwise feel completely dominated in discussion and argument by more self-confident and aggressive male comrades. Indeed, the demand for such separate groupings comes out of the earlier history of the women's movement when closed 'consciousness-raising' groups were a tool for creating confidence and trust among women and giving them a belief in their own capacity to contribute to public debate. Similarly, in academic gatherings it seems absolutely essential that there be distinct, perhaps even organizationally separate groups for the study of such objects as 'Women in Literature', 'Women and the Family' or 'Women in the Peasantry' or 'Women in the Industrial Revolution'. However, over time this tendency seems to have become almost universalized, so that there is now not a single subject within the purview of social science and humanities in which conference or seminar organizers are not faced with demands for a discussion of the 'women's aspect' or of 'women's role' in whatever it may be. Now the point here is not that such demands are *a priori* illegitimate but that they are often both made and conceded purely formalistically. Feminists make them because it appears incumbent upon them as feminists to make them, and organizers (particularly if they are men) concede them because they feel it would be 'sexist' and 'reactionary' to refuse. Often they feel that it would be 'sexist' and 'reactionary' even to ask for an intellectual justification of the demand itself. This can occasionally lead to situations where women (and men) gather together to discuss the woman's role in, or view of X, only to find that there is little or nothing to say, or at least little or nothing which is peculiar or unique to women.

A concrete example that illustrates this point well is the demand for a separate organization for women within CND. Now clearly, in so far as such a grouping may be concerned with the status and role of women within CND as an organization and with advancing that status (for example by positive discrimination in election of officers or delegates), it may have a role. However, in so far as it may be seeking a separate or distinct 'women's view' of the bomb or of disarmament, its objective seems purely metaphysical. As an absolute minimum, the only qualification required for joining CND is the desire not to be blown up, and it is not clear that this desire is differentiated either in quality or amount by gender. Such a consideration also leads one to question the relevance of the principle of 'positive discrimination' within CND, i.e. to ask whether, *in the specific context of CND*, the gender of delegates or officers is of any functional significance at all. But this is precisely what I meant in talking of the 'formalism' that has recently overtaken the treatment of 'the women's question' and feminism within radical and left organizations of all types. When the demand for a separate CND organization for women or for positive discrimination in favour of women in delegate elections is made, such issues as the above are not even raised, let alone debated, because it is considered reactionary or sexist to do so.

And thus we are led back to the reflections with which I began this section of the discussion. For the central point here is not an insistence that feminist historians should aim at a total remoulding of the approach to women in history rather than at the construction of a separate 'women's history' (though obviously I do believe that), nor to insist that separate groupings of women within academic and political contexts are justified in this case but not in that. Both these issues must be the subject of continuous debate (and the first certainly is much debated among feminists). The central point is that such debate can and is being restricted by explicit or implicit pressures by feminists on men which renders their raising such issues illegitimate or unacceptable. At its very worst, raising such issues can produce such highly emotional responses that there is an unwillingness to risk 'upsetting' feminist comrades further by raising them again. And yet it is a frequent theme of feminist analyses of the family, for example, that this sort of emotional blackmail of men by women is very often an attempt by women to assert power in the domestic situation which they are denied in virtually all other situations. As such, it is seen as largely pathological, and is certainly both irrational and highly destructive. Its use as a political tool in public is therefore hardly desirable or 'liberated' on any definition of the latter term.

But does any of this really matter very much? Surely the difficulties and complexities of feminist involvement in radical political and intellectual movements, whilst they may be of importance to the tiny minority of men and women who come together in Left gatherings, are a trivial drop in the bucket when compared with the broader tasks which face the feminist and socialist movements as a whole in this country? I think this is so, which is one reason why I suggested that the first set of difficulties facing the feminist movement (relationships between the feminist minority of women and the non-feminist majority) was of far greater political importance, certainly at the moment. If the essential feminist analysis is correct and all women in our society suffer an oppression which takes real and obvious forms and which is experienced and recognized (albeit in very partial and confused ways) by women, then the political potential of the feminist movement is enormous. It possesses a vast constituency and a capacity to revolutionize a whole set of private and public social relationships in our society. To repeat then, if the behaviour or social characteristics of the feminist movement lead to such an opportunity being squandered, this would be a tragedy of immense proportions. Since I believe that the essential feminist analysis is true, I do believe that both the opportunity and the loss if the opportunity is not taken are real enough.

For this reason, I think that the problems of relationships

between feminists and men within radical movements are secondary issues affecting comparatively few people and can certainly be 'lived with' if necessary. However, it is important to recognize that there is a link between this problem and the first, more important and politically pressing one. For the latter problem is just another reflection of that isolation and ghettoiz-ation which, all denials to the contrary, affect the feminist movement just as profoundly as all other socialist and radical movements in Britain at the moment.

To put it most cruelly, a vast amount of intellectual and emotional energy is invested in the subtlest minutiae of feminist mobilization and male response within radical movements because it is not and cannot be invested effectively in the task of reaching the millions of 'sexist' women and men outside such movements. We are confronted here with a perfect example of what psychologists term 'displacement activity': the sound and fury of a phoney war whose intensity is all the greater because it has to contain the energies which should but cannot be expended on a larger canvas.

And to return to an earlier time, a part of this displacement activity is a gradual but profound loss of perspective, so that in the myopia of internecine debate the marginality and peculiarity (sociologically speaking) of all the participants (women *and* men) are overlooked or even denied. For feminists, as for most other radical minorities in this country, the essential problem is how to move out of the ghetto and to regain a sense of perspective on the extent and nature of the real tasks confronting their movement. Doing the former would in my view produce the latter almost automatically.

It is not, therefore, that the feminist movement lacks a clear sociological base or identity. There is, at least, the impression that the majority of consciously feminist women (a) are aged between *c.* 25 and 40, (b) have had some exposure to higher or further education, usually in the social sciences or humanities, (c) work, outside the home, mainly in public sector service activities (teaching, social and community work, central and local government), and (d) are generally recognizable by certain styles of dress (including a plethora of badges) and speech, especially a wide range and variety of vocabulary which usually distinguish people who have had some higher education. (This sort of characterization is more accurate than the usual description of feminists as 'middle class'. Some feminist women are not 'middle class' in origin and, in common with most other sorts of radicals, feminist women are usually anxious to eschew at least the most obvious signs of 'middle classness' as that term is usually understood, culturally, in Britain – in terms of dress and accent.)

So the problem is not that feminists lack a base or a clear sociological identity. The problem is rather that that identity is patent to virtually all other women, and forms a considerable and durable barrier between feminist women and other women. This barrier is twofold. It derives first from the general sociological characteristic which feminists share with the rest of what is still a small minority of women in general – the characteristic of being highly educated. This characteristic alone sets feminist women apart from the bulk of both 'working-class' *and* 'middle-class' women. Secondly, however, feminist women add a further layer to the barrier by adding characteristics – particularly of dress and general appearance – which are specifically characteristic of feminist women of high education, and not necessarily shared with other women with such education.

Why are these characteristics barriers? They act as barriers for a reason that feminists themselves were very sensitive to in their critique of traditional Left movements; they are both intimidating to women who do not possess them and they present feminist women to other women as alien and other ('strange', 'odd', 'weird'), which provides a perfect rationalization for not listening to what feminists say or labelling it and dismissing it as 'weird', 'intellectual', 'extreme'. In short, we come at this point to a problem that feminists share with all radical and socialist movements in this country, and that feminists do share it seems particularly ironic and sad, given what is perhaps the movement's most profound new insight on politics in general – that 'the personal is political'. The problem may be simply stated. It is that if one is endeavouring to persuade another person of the wrongness or even the partiality and confusion of their views and attitudes, one is engaged in an activity that is personally extremely threatening to the other person. For this reason alone, if one is to have any hope of success in such a venture, one must first build a relationship with the other person which will provide enough trust and mutual respect to make possible such an extremely threatening exercise. The more profound and far reaching the changes of attitudes and behaviour which are involved, the more important these ingredients of trust, respect, even affection become. However, a major impediment to the formation of such relationships, indeed even to the making of initial personal contacts, are stereotypes. For the effect of stereotypes, or rather of negative stereotypes, is to convince one that one already 'knows' what the other person is like, and on the basis of that stereotype one 'knows' that he/she/they 'aren't my kind of person/people'. 'They' have 'nothing in common' with 'people like me'. It is precisely because stereotypes have this very marked blocking effect that the press and media try so assiduously to propogate them about all radical movements, including feminism. But feminists, like other radicals and leftists, must recognize that in part our own activity actively feeds such stereotypes, or that, at the very least, we have not made behaviour which would actively blow them up or confuse them into a central element in our political activity.

For many men and women in this country have *only* these stereotypes by which to 'recognize' radicals of all types. If one does not dress in a manner that they expect or use a 'jargon' that they can label and identify and is found in all sorts of places (from golf clubs to women's institutes) where radicals are not 'supposed' to be found, one can actually say and do all sorts of things of which note will be taken. That is, once certain stereotypical expectations are thrown into confusion, that confusion and the 'openness' that it induces can provide opportunities for creating relationships (genuine ones, not instrumental ones) which may, slowly, have political consequences.

These reflections are of particular importance for feminists if what I have identified as the 'fundamental' feminist position is essentially correct. For if all women experience daily some aspect of the discrimination and disability that they suffer as women, it follows that, simply in the forming of relationships with other women and in interacting with them, these experiences and reflections upon them will be shared. These may range from dissatisfaction at the level of one's husband's role in child care, to tiredness induced by working outside and inside the home, to the lack of sympathy and understanding shown by a male GP or priest. The task therefore for feminists is to expand systematically the range of such contacts and interactions, and thus of the opportunities that they provide.

Of course, a good deal of this happens already. For feminists are not simply defined by their feminism. They are also next-door neighbours, single parents, working mothers, sisters, shop and launderette users, etc. But the problem is that in the feminist movement as such, this kind of activity (the activity which is part of life as it were) is not defined as quintessentially political or feminist activity. In my terms, and very ironically, most of what is defined as feminist movement activity is 'ghetto' activity, from marches and demonstrations, to conferences, to setting up and running very narrowly used 'women's centres'. But if feminists (and others) are to get 'beyond the fragments', it is precisely this redefinition of what political activity is and what it implies for the way in which feminists and other radicals should behave that should be the primary concern. One implication may as well be made explicit. An essential prerequisite of a successful move out of the ghetto and into the world of the vast majority who are 'neither black nor poor nor radical' for feminists as well as other radicals may be, quite consciously, giving up the outward signs of 'inward grace'. That is, one would, at least on certain occasions, dress and behave in ways which would commend one to a leading light in the townswomen's guild or a well-dressed group of working women out for the evening.

But is this not the worst kind of patronization? Is it not also the worst kind of self-emasculation? After all, patterns of dress, the use of perfume and make-up are not 'trivial' things. Both form important parts of the feminist critique of the role which women are given to play in our society. Their rejection therefore is not simply an act of aesthetic preference, but an important political and symbolic statement. This is certainly true and I am certainly not suggesting that feminists revert to 'feminine' stereotypes as a lifestyle in order to gain greater effectiveness. Certainly, when one is in the company of 'sisters' and others who share one's premises (as well as when one is simply relaxed and being with friends) one should dress and behave as it pleases one (in fact I believe this happens already to a large degree). But in presenting oneself to a wider world of women and men, it is as true in radical politics as in everything else that 'it ain't what you do, it's the way that you do it. That's what gets results.' A general feminist obliviousness to this point – a point beknown to every sales executive in the world – always astounds me, because it seems so obviously to be entailed by the principle that 'the personal is political', that the political is also personal. In endeavouring to change minds and hearts one must first demonstrate a respect for the kinds of behaviour and outward forms which are so often so central to the self-image and self-esteem people must maintain even as they change. If one is oneself in the role of the person who is trying to induce or encourage such change, then if there is a choice between appearing to threaten that self-esteem and self-image and making certain tactical changes in order to make sure that one does not, one must choose the latter course if one wishes to have any chance of being effective. It is not therefore a choice between right and being effective. It is a question of finding ways to be right and effective, even if some of those ways are personally rather uncomfortable.

It is precisely because such issues and the changes which they imply are so hard to confront that feminists, as well as other radicals, fall back on a sort of desperate determinism. Whatever the Women's Movement does, its support will grow because somehow, automatically, the oppression all women suffer will push them sooner or later to feminist conclusions. But just like the 'big bang' theory of capitalist collapse favoured by some Marxists (see Chapter 1) all that one can say to this is that the evidence is overwhelming that it just ain't so. Oppression may be experienced and discrimination seen and recognized, but it is as easy to 'explain them away' as to seek to understand and resist them. Therefore, it does matter profoundly what the Women's Movement does and how its members behave; and the evidence is that its current activities and behaviour mean that even when the feminist movement does grow, it grows within very particular and sociologically atypical categories of women. This in turn, I would argue, means that its chances of expanding beyond these boundaries diminish with every new recruit coming from within them, because such sociologically specific growth gives the movement a stronger and stronger sectional identity, an identity that is alien to the majority of women.

All this may seem very harsh. I can only say that virtually all of the criticisms which have been made here of feminism apply even more powerfully to other Left groups and movements in Britain. Indeed, as I said at the beginning of this chapter, I conceive it as only applying to feminism the principles and lessons that feminists first brought to socialism in Britain and that I found so exciting and true when I first encountered them.

It is a central theme, implicit or explicit, of this book that in a sense socialism is too important to the future of humanity to be left simply to socialists. Similarly, I feel that feminism is too important for both women and men and too central to the construction of any society which could meaningfully be termed a real democracy (socialist or otherwise) to be left simply to feminists. Thus the fundamental support for both the principles and achievements of feminism over the last decade or so expressed at the beginning of this essay was no mere stylistic or tactical device or some kind of formal genuflection. It is rather the foundation from which the subsequent criticisms commence.

Precisely because the feminist movement has achieved so much in such a relatively short space of time, and because I am optimistic that there remains an enormous potential for its further growth, it seems absolutely vital that it should not, for want of some self-assessment and reflection, run into a dead end.

5 / Pre-emptive unionism: a possible way forward for socialism in Britain

'First of all they were very well organised . . . secondly, what made it especially exciting was, here was a group who had done enough work to anticipate what was going to happen to them and wanted to see what could be done. Others, like shop stewards at Ferranti's and Alfred Herbert's, had come to me at the last minute saying their firm had gone bust and what could I do. But here was a group who had gone further and had some idea of what needed to be done.' (Tony Benn speaking of his meeting with Lucas Aerospace Shop Stewards Combine Committee, November 1974)

'It will change society.' (Jim Cooney, a member of the combine committee, commenting upon the adoption of the alternative corporate plan by the combine in January 1976. Cooney had argued against the plan and later split from the committee over it.)

Officially there are three and a half million people out of work in Britain; unofficially there are a great many more, especially if account is taken of women workers forced back into the home but not registering as unemployed. Many of the unemployed are young, and of these a disproportionate number are black or brown. Meanwhile, industrial output, though currently (January 1983) rising fractionally, is at its lowest level since 1968 and investment is stagnant. A Tory administration committed to monetarism has made savage attacks on many areas of public spending, particularly in those areas (public housing, education, welfare services) on which the poorest people in our society are most dependent. In addition, its hostility to organized labour and its attacks on trade union rights and powers are the most ideologically explicit, strident and sustained of any administration in post-war Britain. Several of its spokesmen have come close to an open public declaration of their willingness to use mass unemployment as a tool to weaken unions and stimulate 'realism' in wage bargaining.

In such a situation one would not need to be a particularly 'vulgar' Marxist to expect a sharp polarization of political conflict along class lines with both the unemployed and unionized workers moving to support Left alternatives in the face of the most virulent and sustained right-wing assault of the post-war period. However, nothing like this has happened or seems likely to happen.

On the contrary: it is clear that the popularity of the Labour Party electorally is in almost exactly inverse proportion to the strength of the Left within it. Realization that this is the case (indeed it is confirmed by virtually every public opinion poll) is the principal factor behind the current (December 1982) assault on the Militant Tendency within the party, and will almost certainly go further with an attempt also to marginalize the Bennite Left. This will, however, be more difficult given the strength of the Bennite tendency in the Labour Party's constituency organizations, and may indeed be the principal obstacle in the way of the attempt by the Right to re-establish the Labour Party's image as a safe and 'respectable' centre-left social democratic party which can 'safely' be entrusted with governmental power.

For anyone of a Left political persuasion (from the Left of the Labour Party onwards) this is a gloomy picture and one which ought to stimulate a quite fundamental reappraisal of Left political thinking. It is certainly true that beneath this flood tide to the Centre and away from Left politics of all forms, there are some counter-currents from which we may take some solace. Of these, the three most significant are the spectacular renaissance of the Campaign for Nuclear Disarmament focused upon the dangers posed by a new generation of 'strategic' nuclear weapons, the growth in numbers and influence of the women's movement and the rise of a popular base for Left Labour politics, both within the Labour Party and trade union movement. As I have already indicated, it seems to me that all three of these movements share a similar class and generational base. That is, they all draw disproportionate support from relatively well educated white-collar workers, predominantly in the public sector, and predominantly in service occupations. It also seems that virtually all the people involved are in the same broad age band from the mid-twenties to the mid-forties, and are indeed products of the 1944 Education Act and of the whole post-war expansion of state-provided secondary and higher education.

So, counter-currents exist and their class and generational composition in an interesting and significant feature. It suggests a considerable capacity for future expansion. But this should not blind us to the obvious fact that in a parliamentary democratic system with a universal franchise, the Left (however broadly defined) is crucially handicapped by its sheer lack of numbers. Though it can occasionally throng the streets of London with a mass demonstration, it does not have enough support, nor indeed enough geographically concentrated support, to matter a bag of beans in a general election.

But more significant, and certainly more depressing in its implications, than the above obvious but frequently disparaged fact is that the particular class and generational composition of radical politics in Britain has weakened its appeal for the working class as a whole. Nowhere is this more obviously apparent than in the Labour Party, where the ideological gap between the 'average' party activist and militant and the 'average' Labour voter has never been wider. The perception by Labour voters that the Labour Party is dominated by people who are both sociologically and ideologically distant from them has certainly been a powerful factor in defections to the SDP and in withdrawal of support in the polls and at by-elections. A similar phenomenon, however, is to be observed among trade unions where there is an equally huge gap between administrators and activists and the rank and file, the former often being well to the left of the latter across a wide range of social and political issues. The 'militancy' of the rank and file, in so far as it exists at all, is restricted purely to questions of wages and conditions. It is this gap which partly at least explains the frequently reproduced findings of public opinion polls that even union members agree with propositions about 'overly powerful' trade unions damaging 'the national interest'.

But it is important to appreciate how complex all these tendencies are. For if these slow but fundamental structural shifts in the occupational and sexual composition of the working class in Britain have produced a new class base for an expanded radical politics, such shifts have also weakened the hold of 'traditional' Labour loyalties on the class as a whole. It is probably true, for example, that the ideological perspective and occupational composition of an active branch of the Labour Party or trade union was always somewhat different than those of its wider constituency. But a whole range of shifts in the structure of the working class has now weakened the willingness of followers to be trusting, loyal, 'election-booth fodder', for the leadership. I can gesture at some of the factors here: rising educational levels, greater occupational complexity and mobility within the working class, weakening of older class-based communities in the traditional heavy industries, some weakening of patriarchy within the family which had traditionally made women's voting patterns heavily determined by their menfolk. All these things can be enumerated, and many of them may be considered as quite desirable long-term trends with positive implications for democratic life (see Chapter 1), even if their short term implications are damaging to the Left. But though I can enumerate, I am sure that this enumeration is incomplete, and that I do not understand all the subtle and variously weighted combinations of these factors which have made the British electorate ever more 'volatile' (as the political commentators say) in its voting behaviour. I am not in fact sure that anyone fully understands these shifts or their long-term implication or indeed their regional variations (which produce yet further complications), but I am sure that we must try to do so, if Left political understanding is to move beyond the essentially static class categories in which it is still ensnared in theory and practice.

There is at least one more factor which could have been added to the list above to explain the weakening hold of Labour politics on the British working class, a factor which is frequently adduced by the Left itself – the role of the mass media. It is clear that denied access to effective means of mass communication, the Left in Britain (and here I include everyone from the Bennite Left in the Labour Party to all the Left and radical sects) is severely handicapped in current political conflicts. Conversely, the powerful and multifarious channels of communication which are so eagerly and frequently open to ideas of the Centre and Right help to give certain of those ideas the status of an almost unchallengeable conventional wisdom among all classes in our society. Indeed, so massively biased are the means of mass communication towards the ideas of the Right and Centre, that it is possible to make out a case in terms of classical democratic values ('a free and fair competition of ideas') for some reforms in both the press and media. Such a case is presently being most persuasively formulated by the Campaign for Press Freedom (among other organizations) and such campaigns should have the full support of everyone on the Left who cares for a full and varied democratic life.

Yet in the end I am not convinced that the role and power of the mass media can bear all the weight which some sections of the Left (particularly within the Labour Party) would like to place upon it, in accounting for their current weakness. My doubts spring from the simple reflection that there is nothing new here. Since the beginnings of mass democratic politics in this country in the late nineteenth century, the Right has always dominated the means of mass communication and the Left has always had to struggle to make its ideas heard. If this were not true Marx could hardly have remarked nearly a century ago that 'the ruling ideas of every epoch are the ideas of its ruling class', the precise import of which was that ideas are 'ruling' ideas because the ruled (as well as the rulers) believe in them. Domination of the means of mass communication is one (but only one, and perhaps not the most important) means by which ruling ideas rule. It is perhaps arguable that changes in the technology of mass communication and particularly the substitution of electronic media for the printed word as the major means of communication of political ideas have made 'the competition of ideas' even more firmly weighted in favour of those with capital, whilst monopolistic tendencies in newspaper production and distribution have had the same effect on printed media. There is clearly much to be said for such arguments, as for the closely related argument that modern mass media are particularly congenial to highly centralized control. To that degree, quantitative changes since the late nineteenth or early twentieth century may have culminated in a qualitatively changed situation. For example, cost constraints in and of themselves now effectively shut out the Left from controlling its own mass media, leaving aside overt political bias and manipulation in the existing media.

Nonetheless one cannot escape from the conviction, rooted in historical observation, that when Left ideas answer to popularly felt needs or spark popularly felt resentments, they can spread with astonishing rapidity and effectiveness. They did so, for example, in the General Strike, in the armed forces during the war, during the miners' strike of 1974 and are doing so again in the current campaigns of CND. At such moments access to the mass media can be 'forced', whatever its controllers may think or feel about the matter.

I therefore conclude that though the problem of the mass media is real, and at deeper ideological levels (in the formation of racial or gender stereotypes and images for example) the insistent daily drip of distortion and illusion may be particularly pernicious, the current weakness of the Left cannot be blamed on this factor alone. Much more important in my view – and indeed facilitating the role of the media in its discrediting of the Left – is the fact that both the Left and the working class in Britain are trapped in a contradiction which is not perceived by the latter at all, and is but imperfectly understood by the former. As this contradiction works itself out, however, it always ends by discrediting the Left in the eyes of its supposed constituency.

To make clear what I mean it is necessary to abstract a little from complex reality and to conceive matters at the level of the entire British economy and of the entire British working class, at least for the purpose of presenting the fundamental idea. Qualifications and complications can be added later.

It is accepted among many observers of the British economy of all political and ideological persuasions that the period since the Second World War has seen a more or less continuous fall in the rate of profit, especially in the industrial sector. Explanations of this agreed phenomenon vary widely and, on the Left in particular, an orthodox Marxist argument from 'the rising organic composition of capital' is at odds with an interpretation which places much greater stress on relative scarcity of labour, enhanced union bargaining power and international competition (restricting capitalist scope for raising prices in line with wages). In keeping with the broadly political bent of this book, I do not wish to enter into this debate here. I want simply to note that against this background a repetitive and damaging (for the Left) pattern has been enacted which has reached its logical culmination in Thatcherism and the current general retreat and disarray of the whole trade union movement. The pattern is broadly as follows: workers press for improvements in pay and conditions, using methods, including strike action, which are strongly and indeed routinely supported by the Left. Whether because of inadequate investment or international competition or incompetent management (in this context it doesn't matter why, though in others it does), these wage increases occur at the cost of profits. To a degree, and particularly in a period of world capitalist expansion, this impact on profits can be offset by inflationary price increases. In so far as these price increases affect working-class living standards, the Left tends to oppose these too, demanding price and dividend controls, etc. However, in a period of world recession with severely sharpened international competition for stagnant or shrinking markets the 'inflationary' protection of profits (always only partially successful in any case) is no longer open. Any attempt to use it makes the individual firm 'uncompetitive' and produces losses, closures, unemployment, and so on. In this situation, employers are left with only the 'classical' way out to protect profits, i.e. they must reduce wage costs and increase output. In other words they must increase productivity per worker. Reducing wage costs per unit of output through lay-offs, closures and redundancies carries with it the contradiction that in the short or medium term it further depresses profits by reducing demand. But nonetheless, for the system as a whole, it is rational to risk further reducing the rate of profit (and indeed for some more 'inefficient' sections of capital to go out of business entirely) in the short term in order to restore the essential condition of a higher long-term rate of profit – an increased rate of relative surplus value (or, in orthodox terms, a decreased share of wages in total output).

Leaving aside arcane embellishments relating the money supply or the Public Sector Borrowing Requirement to the rate of inflation, this is the real essence of monetarism. Significantly, it is this aspect of the doctrine – an 'iron law' relating wages to productivity, and a refusal to 'print' wage rises through increases in the money supply – which Mrs Thatcher stresses over and over again. Now the problem for the Left is that, in a capitalist context, her logic is impeccable. As long as the British working class is a subordinated class within capitalism, i.e. so long as all or most workers desire to raise their standard of living within the system, it is true that this can only be done continuously if their productivity is at least equal to, or not markedly short of such working classes as the German, Japanese or American. It is also true that within a competitive world capitalist system, money wage increases which are not matched by productivity increases will simply be inflationary and produce no lasting increases in real standards of living. It is very significant in this context that the British working class, perhaps the most effectively unionized working class in western Europe, despite an almost unequal record of economic 'militancy', has the second lowest level of average real wages in the EEC. Of course, it is not the British working class alone which is responsible for its comparatively low level of per worker productivity: British capital has also played a role in this (see below). But nonetheless, it remains true that in a competitive world capitalist system, so long as its real productivity remains comparatively low, the British working class will experience a comparatively slow growth in its real wage level.

Hence, the oft repeated pattern which I referred to earlier. A section of British workers (in coal, steel, the automobile sector) confronts management with a demand for wage increases. If there are no corresponding increases in productivity, such increases are funded by inflationary means (this was a common enough occurrence in the 'long boom' period from the early 1950s to 1973–74). However, with rising costs and prices, the output of these industries becomes gradually more and more uncompetitive on domestic and international markets, even in periods of expansion, and with the recession the crunch comes and losses rise rapidly. In this situation further demands for wage increases place workers in an 'eyeball to eyeball' situation with management. The latter are able to say, honestly, that they are unable to pay, and indeed that the business cannot survive without redundancies. The crucial moment thus arrives when a section of workers must either accept capitalist rationality and retreat pell-mell or must convert economic demands into political demands for a total change in the economic system. In general neither the working class as a whole, nor any section thereof, wants to change 'the rules of the game' in this way, and so in this situation retreat becomes inevitable. Indeed it is genuinely the only 'rational' course. Hence, such a pell-mell retreat occurs, loudly endorsed by the media as a display of 'responsibility' and 'common sense', leaving Left militants and trade unionists, who have ridden the previous waves of economic militancy to the limit, stranded like beached and flapping whales. In such a situation, too, demands in the *Socialist Worker* or *Morning Star* or *Tribune* for resisting redundancies, taking strike action or occupying factories are apt to seem to most workers as the stand of King Canute before the tide. There seems to be and indeed there is, so long as capitalist rationality is accepted, 'no real choice' in the matter. If the bosses don't have the money, they can't pay can they? If they are making losses, they must lay people off mustn't they? *Yes they must.*

Hence in a severe recession like the current one, workers come to believe that the most that can be hoped for is a set of political and economic policies which face the 'harsh realities' of the need for competitiveness' and 'industrial discipline', but which temper these monetarist strictures with a degree of 'humanity' and welfarism, i.e. more or less the combination currently being offered by the SDP. Leftist demands to 'resist all redundancies' or Bennite formulae which claim to solve the problem through a combination of protectionism, increased state intervention and workers' control hardly seem an answer to workers who are themselves often strongly aware of the overmanned, under-invested, uncompetitive nature of the industries in which they are working. Left solutions seem, and I would argue that they are, simply 'unrealistic' and confused when set against the hard, indubitably logical core of monetarism. Hence such solutions are discredited, a discrediting made worse by the fact that Left trade union militants and others have previously encouraged workers to believe that a continuous militancy over wage increases could be costless, and that employers' talk about 'productivity' and 'competitiveness' was just so much propaganda. Hence capitalist crises habitually render the Left in Britain ideologically naked at the very moment that they send workers to the dole queue.

Thus there is an endlessly repeated pattern for the Left: militancy, advance, confrontation, retreat, discrediting, and then (as the system expands again) militancy, advance and so on. The net result of all this is that one has the worst of all possible worlds. The tragedy of the British working class in fact is that it is neither radical enough nor self-confident enough to wish to change the system, yet it is too well-organized and economically militant to allow it to function 'properly'. Or conversely, it is well enough subordinated ideologically that, when a clear choice has to be made, the boat will not be rocked, but it is not sufficiently well subordinated (as for example the Japanese or German working classes) to get the most, materially, for itself out of rapid capitalist growth. Moreover, as the last two years have shown with a painful clarity, if one accepts capitalist rationality only in a crunch – only, that is to say, when it is forced upon one by recession, losses and bankruptcy – the social and human suffering involved is actually *increased*. It is true, for example, that had the contraction and reconstruction of the British steel industry been planned ahead and undertaken gradually, steel workers and their families and communities could have suffered much less.

It is the last reflection which brings me to what seems to be the germ of an alternative strategy for the Left in Britain. Instead of simply pushing for ever improved wages and conditions within the system in the hope that the necessary limitations on such improvements (especially at periods of capitalist crisis) will somehow 'force' workers over into radical political positions, one might quite consciously offer whole-hearted co-operation to capitalism but demand in return for such co-operation concessions which aim quite consciously to change the fundamental nature of capitalism.

However, in order to do this, it would be necessary for unions to develop a research and planning capacity, by industry and sector, which was at least equal if not superior to that of employers. Thus to take a detailed if hypothetical example: the enormously well-staffed Research and Economic Trends Institute of the Iron and Steel Trades Confederation would have said to British iron and steel employers in the mid- or late 1960s that 'our researchers show a rapidly expanding strip steel capacity in the following countries; given manning and wage levels here and there, and a certain degree of technological backwardness in a lot of our strip steel capacity, we foresee declining competitiveness at home and abroad. We therefore suggest the following phased programme of rundowns and restructuring with increased specialization in these (X) new alloys. In return, however, we demand the following:

(a) redundancy payments of X in the following categories . . .;
(b) retraining schemes of the following types, funded over the following period, with retraining grants of not less than average earnings in the following categories . . .;
(c) housing and removing allowances of X level;
(d) capital grants from BSC for new industries in X, Y, Z communities of X amount;
(e) the following delegates on the Board of Directors with full access to information on profits, investment, sales. These delegates to be responsible to the executive of the Union and re-elected regularly;
(f) the firing and replacement of A, B and C (management personnel deemed incompetent);
(g) a profit-sharing scheme structured as below when profits on capital exceed X per cent.'

Of course unions negotiate redundancy deals with employers at the moment (though scarcely of the scope or form of the type suggested above). But the crucial difference between the situation posited above and what normally occurs at the moment is that the deal outlined above is pre-emptive. It is imagined as taking place before a crisis situation has emerged in the industry, and indeed is conceived as a means of pre-empting or mitigating its effects.

It is also obvious that this type of pre-emptive union activity begins almost immediately to pose the question of managerial prerogatives. What one is in fact advocating is the creation of embryonic 'dual power' in which unions suggest managerial initiatives in order to protect and enhance their members' interests. I conceive that such a model could work in a large part of industry and commerce, but also in the public service, in central and local government, in education and the health service.

Its aim in fact is to induce a situation in which management is not the only force involved in managing, but in which union initiatives are framed in such an overtly 'co-operative' and 'reasonable' form (as for 'the good of the industry/sector/service' as a whole) that management resistance can easily be stigmatized as 'unreasonable', 'authoritarian', 'high-handed', etc. One possible result of such a strategy could be the winning of a permanent position of tactical ideological advantage in capital/labour and management/labour relations.

Of course such a situation of embryonic and growing dual power is inherently contradictory and unstable. By definition such union encroachment on managerial prerogatives, however real the concessions made by unions in return (and to be effective they would have to be real and in the interests of capital), would eventually pose central questions of power and control which would have to be resolved in conflict. But the whole aim of this strategy would be both to ascertain the amount of 'play' for democratic advance which exists in the system prior to this point, and to give workers a taste both of power and responsibility upon which they can build the knowledge and self-confidence to go further, even if 'going further' was known to imply severe conflict.

Such a strategy is also unstable and questionable from another perspective. For it is assumed that well staffed and equipped union research and planning departments could read trends in the national and international economy and produce strategies to meet them, more effectively than management does at the moment. Given the abysmal performance of British management in the steel industry, the motor vehicle, motor cycle, shoe and textile industries, for example, over the last ten or twenty years, unions in these sectors could hardly have done worse. But in the end they would confront the same problem as capitalists – the essentially unpredictable and unstable nature of an international economic system which relies mainly on market mechanisms for most of its macro-level outcomes. But once again the very exploration of this contradiction and the drawing of political lessons from it for further advances in national and international economic planning might itself be highly productive from a socialist point of view.

But why would such a strategy not simply result in co-option of unions by management, their domestication into a managerial arm which absorbs a great deal of worker discontent by taking a minor role in decision-making, but which in the end has no real power to protect worker interests? Would this not simply lead to the creation of 'yellow' or 'house' unions, the playthings of management, which would have to be supplanted by 'Solidarity'-type mass movements from below or – more likely in the British context – by unofficial 'wildcat' union activity? The answer to this is that co-option is a real danger, and that much would depend on the quality of the leadership in the unions involved, and, most crucially, on the degree to which the rank-and-file could exert control over both negotiators, managerial delegates, and indeed over the research and planning personnel. In a sense, in order to work as organizations for socialist advance and not of capitalist co-option these unions would require what it is the aim of such a strategy to produce – a sophisticated, informed and disciplined membership, deeply committed to playing a part in more and more of the decisions which affect their life. Since it is a central thesis of this book that in general no such working class exists at the moment, in Britain or anywhere else, we have a contradiction. This contradiction may be resolvable, however, not in abstract argument, but in activity. In beginning to create such union research and planning departments, and in trying to explain to members what they would do and how they would function, in involving the rank-and-file in their activities, as collectors and providers of information, one begins in practice to create, slowly and organically, the conditions to resolve this contradiction.

However, this discussion does not have to remain at such a purely theoretical or hypothetical level. For there has been one attempt to develop a 'pre-emptive unionism' of the sort outlined above – the formation of the Lucas Aerospace Shop Stewards Combine in the period 1969–72, and its production of an alternative 'corporate plan' for the Lucas aerospace factories in January 1976.

The full story of the combine is a long, complex and extremely interesting one, which has been told in full elsewhere. Here I shall simply note some salient features of the experience which bear on the central thesis outlined in this chapter.

(1) The initiative sprang from and was sustained by a group of highly educated and technically skilled workers, many of whom were quite well paid.

(2) The formation of the combine, and above all of the alternative corporate plan, was based upon a research programme initiated by the combine committee, but drawing upon the detailed knowledge and experience of workers at all the Lucas aerospace factories. This allowed information to be obtained which could be used to check that being provided by the Lucas management and to assist in the initial battle against redundancies. It also was the method used to obtain ideas for the 'alternative products' which became the most famous part of the Lucas alternative plan.

(3) The Lucas initiative has led to the formation of two union research and information organizations (the Joint Forum of Combine Committees and the Centre for Alternative Industrial and Technological Systems – CAITS) which function very much in the manner outlined hypothetically above.

(4) The Combine Shop Stewards Committee moved from running a simple 'resistance' campaign against redundancies to the much more ambitious 'alternative plan'. It did so because it realized that so long as the Lucas management could point to declining orders for aerospace products (mainly for defence), a pure resistance campaign could offer no effective political riposte to the management's 'logical' argument that redundancies were regrettable but 'inevitable'. The aim of the corporate plan was

therefore to pre-empt that argument by producing a range of product ideas and prototypes that could be shown to be (a) technically feasible, (b) produceable with Lucas's existing plant and equipment, and (c) commercially viable. Seen simply as a device for resisting redundancy (until the defence market expanded again in 1979–80) this turned out to be highly successful, and placed the Lucas management in a very difficult and embarrassing 'back foot' position. In fact, however, the alternative products of the corporate plan, and indeed the plan itself, turned out to have a great deal more significance and impact than this minimum political gain in bargaining with management.

(5) The responses of the Lucas management to the alternative plan, and especially the accounts of the initial meetings at which the combine committee put forward the plan to management are fascinating in showing precisely how threatening such initiatives are to conventional ideas of management's 'prerogatives'.

The personnel manager's reply was non-committal beyond accepting a copy of the Plan with a promise to consider it and come to a second meeting with a detailed reply. One or two of the technical management expressed genuine interest in the product proposals. However, in the following months it became clear that something other than the product proposals was on the minds of the managers with the power. The decisive factor for them was where the product proposals had come from. Bill Williams, a technical manager for Lucas Aerospace in Birmingham, summed up what was really at stake: 'I'm quite sure personally that the issue was not the viability of the products from an engineering point of view: the real issue at stake was who manages Lucas'.

Several months later, during which time the main plan had been presented to management, Mr Brassington, the personnel manager at the Birmingham site, agreed to a series of local meetings about diversification with representatives of the shop stewards' Liaison Committee. In February (1976), the first – and, as it turned out, last – diversification meeting took place.

Bob Dodd (a member of the Liaison Committee) describes what happened:

> Brassington must have thought it would get nowhere, that our ideas would be pie in the sky and we'd have no technical expertise to back them up. But once we had explained our proposals, the two technical managers there could see what we were getting at. They got into detailed discussions and seemed really interested. Brassington must have got worried because he intervened and poured cold water on the whole thing. He never fixed up another meeting after that.*

Bill Williams was one of the technical managers who had taken the product proposals seriously though not uncritically:

> George Orloff (the other technical manager) and myself had discussed the products as engineers. I don't think that was what was wanted. My expectation was therefore that if they're not able to push the meeting in the way they want, they won't have another one. It was said at the end of the meeting that there would be a second one. I knew it would not take place.*

(6) The experience of forming the combine and then of designing the alternative corporate plan does seem to have built up both knowledge and self-confidence in the way in which I hypothesized above. Indeed it is clear that the combine committee only obtained the self-confidence to design the plan and to challenge management's sole right to manage, as a result of previously successful combine campaigns to resist redundancies and, in particular, to alter the whole structure of the Lucas corporation's pension scheme. The history of the Lucas Aerospace workers' plan is, in good part, a history of an originally sceptical group of shop stewards who were only driven to form the combine in the first place by the need to protect their members' jobs against a

---

* Quotations are from Hilary Wainwright and Dave Elliot, *The Lucas Plan: A New Trade Unionism in the Making?*, London, Allison & Busby, 1982, pp. 113 and 128. The account in this chapter is drawn from this source.

new management structure. But they came to an ever-stronger commitment to the combine and its possibilities when they saw it working and yielding concrete benefits for the workers whom they represented. However, this is an over-simplified way of putting it. Because in effect the combine's 'working' and taking ever more radical initiatives was a result of the growing knowledge and self-confidence of the shop stewards as they endeavoured to make it work. Its 'working', in fact, was nothing other than their collective activity, and the transformation in their attitudes which that activity wrought. As Terry Moran, an AUEW shop steward and member of the combine committee from its beginnings said, 'I must be a completely different person from the person I was six years ago. I used to think everything was Burnley. The Corporate Plan has broadened my horizons unbelievably.'* A concrete example shows precisely how such an attitude change can come about. As a prerequisite of drawing up the alternative plan, the combine committee sent a questionnaire to all its associated factory committees asking them, among other things, for an inventory of all 'their' factory's plant and equipment. This was essential if the alternative products were to be shown to be produceable in Lucas's existing factories.

Mick Cooney from Burnley described the significance of one of these questions:

> They wanted to know what machine tools we had. It was quite amazing that no site knew what they had. The reason for this is that this information was for planning. Now planning production is a fundamental part of running a business. But management does the planning. Workers do the production. To do the alternative Corporate Plan we were having to think as if we were planning. It really made shop stewards sit up.**

* Ibid., p. 112.
** Ibid., p. 89.

However, the experience of the Lucas workers' plan also has some implications for the possibility of a 'pre-emptive unionism' which are somewhat more complex than this. In the first place, it is clear that the formation of the shop stewards' combine itself – and still more its maintenance – had to proceed against the conventional trade union organizations in Lucas Aerosapce rather than emerge from them. In fact the combine was initially formed because shop stewards from a number of separate unions could see no other way of effectively resisting management plans for redundancies. A group of previously independent plants and firms had been unified under Lucas's control in what was in fact a monopolization venture sponsored by the second Wilson government in order to 'rationalize' and strengthen the whole British aerospace industry. A new, centralized, corporate management structure was thus created, which could not be effectively combated by conventional unions based in single 'trades' and in single plants. In effect, the shop stewards' combine was a 'parallel' corporate trade union organization created in tandem with, and in fact somewhat in advance of, the new corporate management structure. In bringing together workers from different unions and plants, and in particular in bringing together both 'shop floor' and 'staff' unions, the combine was enabled to obtain information on management plans and on the effects of such plans in different plants which was vital to its capacity to block or pre-empt management initiatives. However, the inter-union, inter-plant unity which the combine managed to create was always a fragile flower and was also the object of some suspicion among the national level leaderships of several of the constituent unions (especially TASS). Any weakening of this staff shop-floor unity threatened the combine's capacity to act pre-emptively, because white collar staff in particular had access to information denied to shop floor workers, information on managment's plans for rationalizations, redundancies, etc. Thus the 'leaking' of 'confidential' memoranda by sympathetic bosses' secretaries and other white-collar staff allowed the combine to act in anticipation of management initiatives. Here then is a powerful, but alas very rare example of why 'class' action (by all workers) is always much more effective even in a particular firm or organization than action by any one group or section of them. It is more effective precisely because it can be pre-emptive. The Lucas experience also shows, however, how difficult such unity is to create, and once created, to maintain in the face of deeply entrenched (and assiduously fostered) status differences and hostilities, especially between white-collar and blue-collar workers.

Finally, precisely because they were based in sectional 'trade' organizations and because they were concerned purely with wages and conditions, the combine found existing trade union research organizations (even where they existed) of little use and in effect had to create its own. It began, as we have seen, essentially by doing its own research or information gathering from the shop floor and office level. In later years (when it became involved in both the design and the testing of the prototypes of the alternative products) the combine enlisted help in research from sympathetic engineers in the North-east London Polytechnic. (It is now based at the Polytechnic of North London.)

All this suggests that the simple extrapolation from existing union structures and research departments to a pre-emptive unionism which I hypothesized at the beginning of this chapter may be somewhat naïve. It may well be that pre-emptive unionism will require, as a prerequisite, a complete restructuring of union organization, especially if such a unionism is to operate in large and complex organizations (like Lucas Aerospace) which employ workers from several unions. Indeed, one of the lasting consequences of the Lucas initiative has been the interest shown by other workers in similar situations in setting up trade union combines, both for information gathering and for campaigning. The *Joint Forum of Combine Committees*, to which CAITS acts as a Secretariat, has been particularly important in facilitating and supporting such initiatives.

Also, and perhaps most importantly, the model of pre-emptive unionism to which I gave precedence in my hypothetical and schematic account was one which focused on the need for workers to pre-empt and plan for structural changes in their industry or sector which might lead to redundancies in that sector. The idea in fact was to have structural changes carried through in forms and on terms which would obtain the maximum long-term benefits for the workers affected. However, the whole thrust of the Lucas combine's pre-emptive unionism was to resist redundancies rather than to plan ahead for them on their own terms. Anything less than this would undoubtedly have seemed a betrayal of their members to the shop stewards involved. Moreover, it seems that a large part of the popular support given to the alternative plan by the work force in Lucas Aerospace was based on its demonstrated political effectiveness in resisting redundancies. As one might expect therefore, that support tended to diminish somewhat in the period 1979–80 when increased defence spending lifted the threat of redundancies from most of the Lucas aerospace factories.

However, it may well be that in this respect the 'Lucas' brand of pre-emptive unionism is more appropriate to conditions in the 1980s than the model which I outlined at the beginning of this chapter. For those pages were written in late 1980* when it still seemed possible for workers to act in advance of the approaching recession in order to get better terms in what was clearly the onset of a major crisis. That crisis is now with us in full force, and the time for this kind of pre-emption may well have run out. In a sense my initial model of pre-emptive unionism presupposed boom conditions, or at least it assumed conditions somewhat better than a full-scale slump. In the current situation workers may well have virtually no bargaining power to determine the conditions under which sackings and redundancies take place. Therefore the possibility of responding to job losses by finding new products and new activities (as in Lucas) to replace those

---

* In fact they were written before I came across the detailed account of the Lucas plan. Though I had known a little about the latter before reading Wainwright and Elliot, I had not known enough to understand its relevance to pre-emptive unionism.

which have been hit by the slump, or at least to supplement existing activities and thus preserve or create jobs, may well be more attractive and relevant.

In this respect, however, the Lucas plan can seem somewhat confusing because of the particular circumstances in which it arose and the way this influenced its public presentation. The engineers, technicians and designers of Lucas Aerospace were and are highly skilled men (and a few women) who use those skills in order to make sophisticated armaments. It is clear that at least some of the members of the shop stewards' combine felt the moral dilemma which this posed very deeply. Hence, when the alternative corporate plan was drawn up, a lot of emphasis was placed upon finding products which would allow those workers to put their skills to life-enhancing rather than life-destroying purposes. The nature of the alternative products themselves reflects this – portable kidney machines and new types of artificial limbs, radar aids for the blind, a heat pump to provide cheaper and energy-saving forms of domestic heating, a 'road-rail vehicle' for a cheaper and more adaptable form of public transport, improved braking systems, 'telechiric machines' for carrying out manual manipulations by remote control in environments dangerous to human health.

At the time, and subsequently, the combine committee referred to these products as 'socially useful' products, and contrasted them, either explicitly or implicitly, with Lucas Aerospace's existing products. It seems to me that this designation is both too broad and too narrow to be very useful or illuminating politically. It is too broad because depending on how 'socially useful' is defined, any and all products can be claimed to be socially useful. Thus the door was left open for Lucas's management to claim, as indeed it did claim, that armaments are 'socially useful' because they defend our lives, property and way of life from a foreign aggressor. But it is also too narrow because it leaves the impression that the combine designs and prototypes were for products which might not be profitable for capitalism, but served necessary and indeed socially desirable purposes and needs. In this respect, in fact, it claimed too little for the products, some of which have already been taken up and produced commercially by capitalist firms both in Britain and elsewhere, and all of which, arguably, were and are capable of being produced profitably by somebody given the right production and marketing conditions. Again, the particular conditions of Lucas Aerospace may have been misleading here. Lucas's management was lukewarm towards the proposals primarily because of where they came from and the political challenge to management's prerogatives which they posed. But it was also able to say that given the additional investment which the development and commercial production of the products would involve, there was no way in which they could be as profitable as Lucas's existing products, even with reduced defence demand. But this was primarily because government defence contracts were (and are) done on a 'cost plus' basis, i.e on a form of contract which is virtually a 'blank cheque' for the producers as long as they provide the products to the Ministry of Defence's specifications. It is no exaggeration to say that under such cirumstances virtually nothing, no set of alternative products, could have been as profitable for Lucas as defence products. But that is not to say that the alternative products would not have been profitable enough for some other firms, quite profitable enough to interest them in their commercial development – and indeed this has happened.

This is significant because in the current situation it carries important implications. For these ideas and prototypes – and indeed others – can be developed to provide alternative and profitable (i.e. commercially viable) products either for workers facing redundancies or closures in their existing work, or indeed to provide employment for the unemployed. There does not necessarily have to be a direct conflict between producing things which are socially useful (in the sense of fulfilling important human needs, especially for the sick, the old or the poorer in our society) and producing things which will provide commercially viable and long-lasting employment in the capitalist market place. Of course there may in particular cases be such conflicts (produced for the road-rail vehicle, for example, by the general anti-public transport policies of the Tory government), but even then other domestic purchasers (e.g local authorities) and export markets may provide alternative outlets. The important thing from a socialist point of view is that the research and development of these products and indeed their production should occur in non-capitalist forms of organization, i.e. in research and development organizations run and controlled by skilled working people, and in workers' co-operatives and other forms of enterprise which try to dispense with or mitigate traditional hierarchical forms of organization and management. This is quite apart from designing and using other types of 'workers' plans in pre-emptive attempts to protect or create jobs in existing firms and capitalist organizations.

All this then suggests, at least in outline, a possible line of immediate advance for pre-emptive unionism in the present recession. For CAITS should not be a small, over-worked, underfunded organization of four people eking out a precarious existence in the North London Polytechnic. Nor should the Forum of Combine Committees be a similarly underfunded organization dependent upon small amounts of voluntary and union funding and the assistance of CAITS. Both of them should be set within the context of a large and well-funded research, development and project assistance organization or organizations, obtaining money both from the TUC, individual unions, local authorities and anybody else who is sympathetic. Such an organization would design, test and develop alternative products, conduct market research and feasibility studies and assist and fund attempts at producing and distributing these products in forms of enterprise controlled by working people. Thus could pre-emptive unionism take significant form and shape even in this difficult time, and gain credibility in the best way possible, by contributing both to the reduction of unemployment and to an improvement in the quality of life in our society.

Looking beyond the immediate future, however, it is almost

certain that if and when a Labour government or a Labour/SDP government returns to power in Britain, it will want, sooner or later, to negotiate a 'wages policy' (i.e. wage restraint) with the unions. It is my view that the unions should assent to such a policy but in return for a range and type of concessions which go far beyond the usual formal, unimplemented (and arguably unimplementable) demands for control of prices and dividends. Clearly such demands could embrace in addition macro-level policy demands on pensions, health and welfare provision, unemployment, etc., and there are ample precedents for this. But I have in mind a much more radical set of demands formulated by individual unions in individual sectors and industries in which long-term wage bargains are traded for very precise demands on investment policy, marketing, health and safety conditions, manning levels, retraining, an 'open books' policy. It could be the aim of a much strengthened research and planning capacity in each and every public and private sector union to research such demands prior to (and indeed in order to control) national-level negotiations. The essence of the matter is really very simple. If the British working class is to sell itself to capitalism, it must sell itself in a planned, thought-out and expensive fashion; in a fashion which, as its conditions are met, explores the limits of the concessions which capitalism can make without changing its fundamental nature. The central plank in this latter part of the strategy is that the class should sell its co-operation in making capitalism in Britain more competitive and efficient not simply in return for material benefits, but in return for increasing rights to control and decision-making – in return for power, in short. For demands to be structured in this way they would have to be formulated by socialists, and supported by increasing numbers of self-conscious socialists within the working class as a whole. Conversely, however, it is the aim of this strategy to help create these increasing numbers of self-conscious socialists as the contradictions it creates are explored.

The single most difficult aspect of this strategy is precisely that it is pre-emptive. Thus in the hypothetical steel example at the beginning of this chapter, workers would have been asked to give up their jobs (albeit into extremely generous retraining and redeployment schemes) before there was any strict need (i.e. the crunch period of massive losses) for them to do so. This is the hardest thing of all to ask. Workers typically and understandably demand that their unions protect jobs (even jobs which have been made technologically redundant) up to the moment when, without a complete change in the political and economic system, such jobs 'cannot' be protected any longer. There is no doubt in this context that it is the genuinely democratic nature of unions (their tendency to be dominated, in their central functions, by the wishes of their mass membership) which welds them to this essentially short-term rationality. Better a job in the hand than a potential one, no matter how rosily painted, at the other end of a retraining scheme. Similarly, many capitalist and state employers are unwilling to attempt to enforce redundancies against union resistance until they absolutely have to, i.e. until 'the market' forces them to it.

So it is a massive psychological break that is being striven for here, and it is absolutely vital to be clear about the essence of this break. For the British working class (and therefore British trade unions) as much as the bourgeoisie is convinced that 'managers must manage'. If there are redundancies to be made, 'it is up to the bosses' to do that. Above all, 'it is up to the bosses' to relate wage increases to productivity and to sack people in order to keep that relationship in being. In fact it is only by a total and whole-hearted acknowledgement of the legitimacy of this, the management's exclusive domain, that trade unions can claim their restricted but exclusive domain in parallel – the defence and advancement of their members' wages and conditions.

Jim Cooney, therefore (see the quotation at the head of this chapter), was no mere isolated 'reactionary'. In dividing from the rest of the Lucas shop stewards' combine at the precise moment when they moved from traditional trade union activity as he understood it (fighting redundancies, campaigning for better wages, conditions, pension schemes) into an initiative which he felt would 'change society', he was echoing the views not only of the vast majority of trade union members in this country, but the bulk of the organized trade union movement as a whole. And of course he was right; the broad-scale adoption of such a pre-emptive unionism does threaten to 'change society', and it does this by threatening to infiltrate across that line between those who manage and those who are managed, those who make crucial decisions and those who carry them out and bear their consequences (whether good or ill). The negative reaction of the Lucas management to this particular attempt is, I would hazard, a fairly accurate predictor of the response of virtually all the power-holders in our society to any and all attempts to cross that line, or even to smudge it a little. However, the fact that such attempts do produce reactions like this, even or especially when they are presented as and indeed are 'reasonable' and 'sensible', 'for the good of the company/industry/country as a whole', is a sure sign that one is hitting where it hurts. The line is strongly and instantly defended because it is a line of power and thus well worth crossing (and defending). I am suggesting that the immediate aim of socialist strategy in this country should be to infiltrate as many troops across that line in an many places as possible – from factories to furnaces, local government to department stores, publishing houses to insurance companies, architects' offices to armed services, in what would be the start of a continuing 'war of position' to alter the fundamentally élitist assumptions and activity upon which our society, like all parliamentary democracies, still depends.

For if anything that I have said above has been clear, it must be obvious that this traditional trade union principle – of mutually reserved and recognized territory – is a profoundly anti-socialist principle. To begin with, at a purely pragmatic level in the British case it is simply a false principle. The management of British Steel, British Leyland, the British motorcycle and electronics industries could not 'be trusted' to manage. They manifestly and abysmally failed to exercise their managerial function efficiently or successfully, and in a capitalist world their failure is openly attested by the crucial, indeed the only, test – they were out-competed. The moral is clear: if you 'trust the management to manage' you can't complain if you suffer when they cock it up. Secondly, 'trusting the management to manage' is, just like the parallel political principle of 'trusting our politicians to govern', a sign of that lack of self-confidence which marks a subordinate class as subordinate. If workers cannot conceive that they could manage, if indeed they are relieved to be able to restrict their own activity to demanding more when there is more to be had, then they can never be a ruling class – that dissolution of class rule into a rule by a majority so large that it is effectively a self-imposed social regulation (which is the essence of the transition to socialism for Marx) can never occur.

And yet here we have the paradox. For the central issue of economic policy in all advanced capitalist societies today is that of wage regulation – the need to keep wage rises broadly in line with productivity increases in order to ensure sustained growth without inflation. Monetarism is the capitalist class's response to the conviction that such regulation cannot be attained 'voluntarily' under conditions of full employment. Yet it is also clear that wage restraint cannot be maintained over the long term in an oligopolistic economy with a highly unionized and compartmentalized labour market without a continuing level of mass unemployment that would threaten the very political stability of capitalism, or at least would require the drastic abridgement or even ending of democratic freedoms.

It is quite likely therefore that after the monetarist experiment, advanced capitalist economies will return to Keynesian demand management and 'pump priming' for one more, and perhaps final, experiment with more 'moderate' solutions. In doing so, they will once again confront the necessity of winning mass working-class compliance with wage restraint, and various forms of 'social contract' will be born again. In confronting this problem, advanced capitalist economies are simultaneously confronting the most acute contemporary form of what Marx regarded as capitalism's central contradiction – the ever more 'socialized' nature of production and consumption under capitalism and the private appropriation of the profits of that production.

In short, capitalism in Britain may not need a 'responsible' and self-disciplined working class in order to survive. In the end, dictatorial solutions are always a possibility. But it is conceivable that capitalism in conjunction with parliamentary democracy needs such a class in order to survive.* We may therefore see, in the not-too-distant future, a crucial historical moment in which the British working class has an opportunity to extract major, indeed transforming, changes in the capitalist system in return for its co-operation. Yet it will only be able to seize that opportunity if it has the self-confidence to perceive it and to conceive it as takeable, and the self-discipline to exercise self-control and to deliver its side of the bargain. There seems then a conflict between the opportunities which exist and the readiness of a long-subordinated class to grasp them. It is suggested in this essay that the construction of a pre-emptive unionism could be both a means of commencing that transformation and of creating the self-confidence without which it cannot occur.

The central determinant of its ability to fulfil this dual role would be the extent to which the mass of union members could become involved in the formulation of the pre-emptive plans and strategies which are formulated, and indeed in the implementation of those strategies. This poses some very difficult questions

---

* This, incidentally, seems to me to be the central flaw in the whole policy and outlook of the SDP. For it is simultaneously wedded to Keynesian economics and to an old-style elitism. The SDP simply assumes that Keynesian economic policies are still, as they have been in the past, unproblematically compatible with a basically Fabian politics in which the majority do what a minority of enlightened humanitarians think is best for them. I am arguing here that even Keynesian policies, to be effective now, under current conditions, require that working people voluntarily accept a degree of responsibility for the welfare of the capitalist system. It is difficult to see why, or even how, they could do that, unless they have a far greater share in economic power. On the whole, however, the SDP leadership seems, if anything, even less prepared to countenance this than their Liberal allies. Conversely, they are very unhappy with monetarist or other more authoritarian solutions to the problem. But you can't have it all ways.

of organization and institution-building. One is thinking here, as I have suggested, of research and planning organizations which reach down into every factory, building site, warehouse and office, and in which members within these units are engaged in providing and collecting information, and indeed in suggesting new areas for research. Moreover, if and when pre-emptive strategies are put to management and accepted, one envisages members being involved in administering retraining schemes, manning consultancy organizations, advising on the use of redundancy payments, supervising rehousing schemes, acting as directorial delegates, staffing worker committees concerned with new investments from plant level to sector level, administering profit-sharing schemes. One would also envisage regular 'turnover' of workers in all these positions to spread the knowledge and experience of decision-making and research as widely as possible. But how precisely this could be done, and what precise forms of organization would be required would depend crucially upon the detailed circumstances of each individual union and industry. The Lucas combine experience suggests that at the very least some reorganization of union structures and much more inter-union linkages within sectors would be required. In the end in fact, as the 'Lucas plan' also clearly demonstrated, the details can be filled in not by an academic at his typewriter but by workers and union activists in action, using the knowledge that their life experience has given them of the circumstances and problem of their particular industry, factory, local authority, service station, or department store.

Thus, although I could possibly go further with practicalities, this is perhaps not the place to do so. Some limited precedents for the type of thing I have in mind exist in the current research organizations of the TUC and of some of the more aware unions such as ASTMS, as well as — and above all — in CAITS and the Joint Forum of Combines. But at the moment these are all chronically underfinanced and staffed, given the kind of tasks which are outlined above, and many unions do not or cannot support even such embryonic research capacities. Perhaps the very first step in such a strategy is convincing members even of individual unions, let alone of combines, of the need for such a capacity and of the need to pay for it. But at the moment this issue of practical steps is less important than the general argument for a fundamental reorientation of Left thinking and activity in the current phase of capitalist development and crisis. I perceive the essence of this change as being a concentration upon, indeed obsession with, the creation of an ever more wide-ranging and varied democratic public life. In that sense the suggestions in this chapter for the creation of a pre-emptive unionism are of a piece with ideas expressed elsewhere concerning the need to 'make' socialism through democratic involvement and to create a self-disciplined and responsible citizenry by creating a citizenry with power. In all the chapters of this book, on feminism, on radical social history, on socialism and the working class, I have wanted to make this obsession central. I have wanted in fact to remarry socialist ideas with much older concepts of *civitas*, or republican 'virtue', of the duties and powers as well as the passive 'rights' of the citizen. Throughout, I have argued for and used a concept of the working class which embraces women and men and which (including all those who do not own or control the means of production, distribution and exchange) incorporates the vast majority of the adults in this country and indeed in Europe and North America.

The issue of the use and nature of union power is only one of these elements in our current situation which I might have chosen. Consumer rights and their enforcement, popular control and checks on government administration, mass access to the currently misnamed 'mass' media, the control by supporters and competitors over sports and football clubs (a particular obsession of mine), women's role in the workplace and in the family. All these issues and others I might have chosen for discussion as well. All are simply different ways (some more and some less important) of coming at the same issue. I chose pre-emptive unionism because it seemed to illuminate particularly vividly the *impasse* in which the Left finds itself, and also to provide one possible way forward. I am also sufficiently traditional in my socialism to believe that issues of economic power, decisions about what is produced and consumed, by whom and how are particularly central to capitalism. Such issues must therefore find an important, though not exclusive place, in our concepts of socialist construction, if only because 'in the last instance' they affect so much

However, although in this chapter I have concentrated upon the possibilities and potentialities of a pre-emptive unionism, I would not wish this to leave the impression that I favour an unalloyed 'workers' control' as the predominant form of institutional democracy under socialism. On the contrary, it seems to me that schematically the most appropriate form of organization for most enterprises would be a tripartite management structure including representatives of the work force, of the consumers of the product or service produced by the organization, and of the local community in which the organization operated. This tripartite form, perhaps with variations in the weight of these three groupings, would seem to me to be as appropriate to factories as to farms, to local government as to insurance companies, to retail stores as to restaurants. I have concentrated upon pre-emptive unionism in this chapter because of its possible potential as a focus for mobilization and advance from the current situation, not because it embodies in itself an ultimately desirable end-state. It should also be clear that I do not in any case believe in 'end-states', merely in staging posts in an always continuing historical process. It is also certain that should such a tripartite management structure ever come into being, it would be continually wracked by conflicts between the three sets of interests involved (producers, consumers, residents), and probably by conflicts within these groups. Needless to say, I would regard such conflicts as inevitable, and indeed as desirable; an integral part of the learning process by which a knowledgeable and self-disciplined citizenry acquires that knowledge and self-discipline.

Conclusions

This last chapter has been somewhat different from the ones which preceded it. Whilst they were concerned primarily with criticizing conceptions of socialism which are still predominant within the Left and with the types of attitudes and activity which typically flow from such conceptions, this last chapter has been rather more concerned with the current political situation in Britain, and with applying it to the conception of socialism which I outlined earlier. It has tried in short to provide at least a sketch of a strategy of advance from where we are now – a 'transitional programme' – or at least an aspect of one, rather than simply a liturgy of principles and broad objectives. If one is not capable of doing this, of making some connection between posited long-term goals and immediate circumstances and objectives, then socialist theory is reduced either to an illuminating but hopeless social criticism or to the mere building of castles in the air, a temporary balm and consolation which soon gives way to an even deeper gloom about current prospects.

Such a transitional programme is also necessary because one needs some bridge from the present to the future and some sense of what the first steps over that bridge might be. Otherwise the gap between what seems required and desirable and what is appears so large as to be totally dispiriting. It can be even more dispiriting if one holds, as I do, that the kind of fundamental social change, the deepening and extending of democracy, at which socialists aim comes only as the result of a slow, con-tradictory and painful historical process. At such moments it is as well to compare the present not with the desired future but with the known past, to remember the Britain which eighteenth- and nineteenth-century reformers and radicals confronted:

> There were inspected in all 6951 houses . . . of these 6565 urgently needed whitewashing within. 960 were out of repair, 939 had insufficient drains. 1435 were damp, 452 were badly ventilated, 2,221 were without privies. Of the 687 streets

inspected, 248 were unpaved, 53 but partially paved, 112 ill-
ventilated, 352 containing standing-pools, heaps of debris,
refuse etc. . . . It often happens that a whole Irish family is
crowded into one bed; often a heap of filthy straw or quilt of
old sacking cover all in an indiscriminate heap, where all alike
are degraded by want, stolidity and wretchedness. Often the
inspectors found in a single house, two families in two rooms.
All slept in one and used the other as a kitchen and dining-
room in common. Often more than one family lived in a single
damp cellar, in whose pestilent atmosphere 12 to 16 persons
were crowded together. To these and other sources of disease
must be added that pigs were kept . . . Gaskell gives the
number of persons living in cellars in Manchester proper as
20,000. *The Weekly Dispatch* gives the number 'according to
official reports' as 12% of the working class. . . . The death
rate is kept so high chiefly by the heavy mortality among young
children in the working-class. The tender frame of a child is
least able to withstand the unfavourable influences of an
inferior lot in life; the neglect to which they are often subjected,
when both parents work or one is dead, avenges itself promptly
and no one need wonder that in Manchester . . . more than
57% of the children of the working class perish before the fifth
year, while but 20% of the children of all classes in the country
die under 5 years of age . . . in general epidemics in Manchester
and Liverpool are three times more fatal than in the country
districts; that affections of the nervous system are quintupled
and stomach troubles trebled, while deaths from affections of
the lungs in cities are to those in the country as $2\frac{1}{2}$ to 1. Fatal
cases of smallpox, measles, scarlet fever, and whooping cough,
among small children, are four times more frequent, those of
water on the brain are trebled, and convulsions ten times more
frequent. (Engels, *The Condition of the Working Class in
England in 1844*, pp.64–6 and 107–8)

At a rolling-mill where the proper hours were from 6 a.m. to $5\frac{1}{4}$
p.m. a boy worked about four nights every week till $8\frac{1}{2}$ p.m. at
least . . . and this for six months. Another, at 9 years old,

sometimes made three 16-hour shifts running, and, when 10, has made two days and two nights running. A third, now 10 . . . worked from 6 a.m. till 12 p.m. three nights, and until 9 p.m. the other nights. Another now 13 . . . worked from 6 p.m. till 12 noon next day, for a week together, and sometimes for three shifts together, e.g. from Monday morning till Thursday night. Another, now 12 has worked in an iron foundry at Stavely from 1 a.m till 12 p.m. for a fortnight on end: could not do it any more. George Allinsworth, age 9, 'came here as a cellar-boy last Friday; next morning we had to begin at 3, so I stopped here all night. Live five miles off. Slept on the floor of the furnace overhead, with an apron under me, and a bit of a jacket over me. The two other days I have been here at 6 a.m. Aye! it *is* hot in here. Before I came here I was nearly a year at the same work at some works in the country. Began there, too, at 3 on Saturday morning – always did, but was very gain (near) home and could sleep at home. Other days I began at 6 in the morning, and gi'en over at 6 or 7 in the evening . . . .

William Turner, age 12 – 'Don't live in England. Think it *is* a country but didn't know before.' John Morris, age 14 – 'Have heard say that God made the world, and that all the people was drowned but one; heard say that one was a little bird.' William Smith, age 15 'god made man. Man made woman.' Edward Taylor, age 15 – 'Do not know of London.' Henry Matthewman, age 17 – 'had been to chapel, but missed a good many times lately. One name that they preached about was Jesus Christ, but I cannot say any others, and I cannot tell anything about him. He was not killed but died like other people. He was not the same as other people in some ways, because he was religious in some ways, and others isn't.' 'The devil is a good person. I don't know where he lives.' 'Christ is a wicked man.' This girl spelt God as dog, and did not know the name of the queen. (Marx, *Capital*, vol.1, pp.258–9 and note)

It was shown that for a family of father, mother and three children, the minimum weekly expenditure upon which physical efficiency can be maintained in York is 21s 8d . . . This estimate was based upon the assumptions that the diet is selected with a careful regard to the nutritive values of various food stuffs, and that these are all purchased at the lowest current prices. It only allows for a diet less generous as regards variety than that supplied to able-bodied paupers in workhouses. It further assumes that no clothing is purchased which is not absolutely necessary for health, and assumes too that it is of the plainest and most economical description . . . No expenditure of any kind is allowed for beyond that which is absolutely necessary for the maintenance of *merely physical efficiency*.

The number of persons whose earnings are so low that they cannot meet the expenditure necessary for the above standard of living, stringent to severity though it is, and bare of all creature comforts was shown to be no less than 7230, or almost exactly 10 per cent of the total population of the city. These persons then represent those who are in 'primary poverty'.

The number of those in 'secondary' poverty was arrived at by ascertaining the *total* number living in poverty and subtracting those living in 'primary' poverty. The investigators, in the course of their house-to-house visitation, noted those families who were obviously living in a state of poverty, i.e. in obvious want and squalor. Sometimes they obtained definite information that the bulk of the earnings was spent in drink or otherwise squandered; sometimes the external evidence of poverty in the home was so clear as to make verbal evidence superfluous . . .

In this way 20,302 persons, or 27.84% of the total population, were returned as living in poverty. Subtracting those whose poverty is 'primary', we arrive at the number living in 'secondary' poverty — viz. 13,072, or 17.93% of the total population. (B. Seebohm Rowntree, *Poverty: A Study of Town Life* (York in 1899). A subsequent survey in 1936 found that 6.8 per cent of the population were still in 'primary poverty' using the 1899 standard: *Poverty and Progress: A Second Social Survey of York*, 1941.)

It is worthwhile from time to time to re-read such sources and to sit and reflect on their implications. It is also worthwhile to peruse one of several dry compilations of historical economic statistics and to find that in 1965 the real value of the average weekly earnings of manual workers in the main industries and services in Britain was seventeen times what it had been in 1855.* One should wonder too at the crude but vivid positivistic contrasts of Ian Gough's table reproduced overleaf.

The point of pausing and reflecting on these obvious but frequently disregarded long-term changes is not to muse on how 'fortunate' the present British working class is compared with its ancestors and how 'grateful' it should be. The point is not even to enter into the heated (and important) debate on the Left about the causes of these changes. For the moment, I am unconcerned with the much-debated issue of whether such changes are 'concessions' rung from capitalism by working-class militancy, or ruling-class 'sops' designed to undermine revolutionary zeal and/or maintain the demand necessary for the realization of surplus value. In any case, it seems to me, as to others, that the whole matter is rather more complex than that.

No: the point is simply to reflect that irrespective of how or why these changes have occured, their consequences are momentous. For it is only a working class which has been released from the physical and intellectual bondage (and from the fear and subservience) that absolute poverty brings which has even the possibility of expanding the horizon of its demands to embrace issues of politics and power. Nothing seems to me – and has always seemed to me – more extraordinary and ridiculous than the persistent and still lingering conviction on the Left that revolutionary zeal is somehow proportionate to the degree and depth of absolute poverty and deprivation. Such a belief lingers in the persistent hankering on the Left to downplay, understate or ignore the material advances that the British working class has

* C.H. Feinstein, *Statistical Tables of National Income, Expenditure and Output of the U.K., 1855–1965*, Cambridge, Cambridge University Press, 1976, table T140, p. 65.

Table 1 State welfare in Britain (*c.* 1860 and *c.* 1970)

	c. 1860	*c. 1970*
Income security	None (except for Poor Law Relief, as in other services)	Old age, invalidity, and survivors' pensions; sickness, maternity and work injury and unemployment benefits (virtually universal scheme). Universal family allowances; national assistance
Medical care	None with the exception of lunatic asylums, vaccination and environmental health services	Comprehensive and free health care for the whole population
Education	None with the exception of education grant (Parliamentary) to religious bodies	Free and compulsory ten-year education; secondary and higher education with maintenance grants
Housing	None	Over one-quarter of all housing publicly provided, largely at subsidized rent; rent regulation in private sector
Proportion of national income spent on state welfare	1–1.5 per cent	24 per cent

Source: Ian Gough, *The Political Economy of the Welfare State*, London, Macmillan, 1979, p.2.

made under capitalism. It is not hard throughout its history to find extraordinary and heroic leaders and intellectuals of the working class who overcome absolute poverty to emerge as cultivated, thoughtful and unremittingly radical men and women. On the whole, however, a large part of the history of the British working class has been the history of William Turner, John Morris, Edward Taylor and Henry Matthewman, a history of men, women and children who were forced to strain all their abilities just to survive or to win a degree of relative and precarious 'upward mobility' and comfort. It is only in the release from those constraints, through a relative (but in long-term historical perspective, quite unprecedented) material prosperity that there is even the possibility of the broad spread of other objectives, priorities and ambitions.

And the second reflection which these documents force upon me is even simpler and more obvious. It is that though there remains both relative and absolute poverty among some sections of British working people in the late twentieth century, none the less working-class people (defined, you will remember, as all those men and women and their families who own no means of production and reproduction save their own labour power) have attained material and social conditions and benefits which were literally inconceivable to their ancestors of a hundred or even fifty years ago, and which represented the limit, and indeed beyond the limit, of what nineteenth-, eighteenth- or seventeenth-century radicals could themselves imagine and demand for 'the people'. If then it seems that the kind of bubbling, conflictual, participatory, self-disciplined, irreverent political and economic democracy which I have outlined as both the means and ends of socialism in the preceding pages is 'fanciful', 'utopian', 'impossible' and above all a long wearisome way away, it is not one whit less so than the National Health Service would have seemed to Gerard Winstanley or the world of Wimpey estates would have seemed to Friedrich Engels. It is not an easy trick, psychologically or emotionally, to instigate and continue political activity holding fast at one and the same time to a conviction of its importance and to a knowledge of how little, comparatively, one may see for results in one's lifetime. It is always easier, at least in the short term, to enlist activists if they can be infused with a conviction of millennial change close at hand. But as we all know too well, the concomitant of such conviction is that when the walls of capitalism do not crumble before the maximalist trumpet, disillusion, cynicism and 'apoliticality' (usually a prelude to conservatism) soon follow. On the other hand, it is equally hard to prevent a determined long haul from degenerating into a mere formal gesturing. The aim of this book has been to suggest that perhaps for all of us it might be a little easier to pull off this difficult trick, to maintain a realism which doesn't kill expectation, and an expectation which doesn't become self-delusion, if we cling to one motto, one slogan, which a good deal of twentieth century thought has aimed to persuade us is false, and which this book has tried to reassert:

'To hope is a rational act, and to act upon that hope maintains the reason for hoping.'

Appendix / politics, economics and intellectuals

The reawakening of an interest in Marxism among western intellectuals over the last twenty or so years has been accompanied, from its very beginnings, by a desire to escape the 'mechanistic', 'economistic' and 'deterministic reductionism' wrought upon Marxism by Stalin, and by the whole Stalinization of the world communist movement from the late 1920s to the late 1950s. In fact the intellectual renaissance of Marxism in the west arose from the rediscovery in the late 1950s of the philosophical writings of the young Marx. In those writings the humanistic theme of 'Man's' self-creation through purposeful 'species-activity' and in particular the philosophical link between Marx's analysis of alienation and his version of the communist future all helped to remould the traditional picture of Marx the 'deterministic' economist and materialist, the enemy of the 'Open Society'.

Once enunciated, these themes have continued to run through western Marxism as a semi-permanent obsession. They have found many different expressions, but perhaps the most important has been the desire to develop a Marxist treatment of politics and the state which does not simply reduce either to the mechanical reflection of class interests. Antonio Gramsci has perhaps been the most important single influence in 'de-economizing' Marxist treatments of the state and politics, whilst the writings of the German 'Frankfurt School' on literature and the mass media have had much the same effect for work on 'ideology'. More recently, the emergence of liberation movements concerned with racial and sexual issues has reinforced even further the concern to see the struggle for the overthrow of capitalism (and even more importantly) for the construction of socialism, as something a lot more complex than simply capitalists v workers. Such movements have insisted upon a frank recognition of the particular and non-class-based forms of oppression and discrimination that black people suffer *as blacks*, the women suffer *as women*, and which gay people suffer *as gays*.

And yet, despite all these attempts to exorcise the ghosts of 'economism' and class 'reductionism' from Marxism (and with them the much more ghoulish figure of Joseph Stalin) they still seem to return again and again and to require yet further exorcism. In a famous polemic published a few years ago, Edward Thompson argued that despite all apparent changes, intellectual 'Stalinism' was still alive and well, and indeed was flourishing in the not so new 'New Left' in Britain; and he attempted yet one more, and unprecedentedly violent, exorcism. Thompson saw intellectual 'Stalinism' as having returned full-fledged to the British Left intellectual scene, through the pernicious influence of Louis Althusser. But the responsibility for introducing the poison of 'Althusserianism' into Britain lay with Perry Anderson and Tom Nairm, who through the journal *New Left Review* had influenced a whole younger generation of Left intellectuals in Britain, and in particular Barry Hindess, Paul Hirst and a number of other young 'structuralist' Marxists associated with the journal *Economy and Society*. There was thus posited a clear line of descent linking 'Messrs Anderson and Nairn' to 'Messrs Hindess and Hirst', and all were represented as one generation marked by its inability to break with the intellectual forms of Stalinism and thus with Stalinism itself. This was so, argued Thompson, whatever the anti-Stalinist protestations of particular individuals and whatever their sectarian allegiances. For the disease went beyond sectarian boundaries (Trotskyism was here just as 'Stalinist' as orthodox communism), and indeed beyond broad tactical or strategic positions on the construction of socialism.

Stalinism, according to Thompson, was nothing less than a whole way of thinking about society, about the role of intellectuals in society, and about the relationship between intellectuals and the working class or other human beings in general. This Stalinist world view to which the intellectual 'New Left' in Britain was still attached was composed, broadly, of the following elements.

(1) An economic reductionist view of society in general, and in particular of 'class' and 'class structure'. The hallmark of this reductionism is a continued attachment to the base/superstructure analogy.

(2) A pursuit of logical rigour and neat, indeed militaristic, conceptualization at the expense of or (in more recent versions – viz. Althusserianism) actually in place of, empirical work.

(3) A marked intellectual élitism as a personal and political style which both reflected and reinforced –

(4) A continued attachment to a Leninist 'vanguardist' conception of the relationship between the working class and intellectuals in which the former (always conceptualized as an 'it' – this is one of the symptoms of intellectual Stalinism) struggles along under a load of 'economism', 'trade-union consciousness', 'empiricism', 'opportunism', and 'reformism' until the latter arrive to pump in some genuine revolutionary theory.

Thus it is clear that for Thompson there was a strong and direct link between the theoretical ideas of the intellectual 'New Left' in Britain and their political practice. According to Thompson, the continued attachment of these intellectuals to a conception of Marxism as some kind of hard, economics-based 'science', led them to an intellectual and political élitism in which only those possessed of this science can form a genuinely revolutionary leadership of the working class. In short, 'economistic' Marxism and Leninist politics go together. Whoever holds to any variant of the former is led to some variant of the latter.

In the rest of this appendix I shall argue that
(1) there is indeed an intellectual élitism and an élitist political practice in the intellectual Left in Britain, but that its origins do not lie in the attachment of such people to an economistic Marxism;
(2) at a purely theoretical level, many of the problems of 'economism' and 'reductionism' are misconceived in any case, not only by Thompson but by very many other people on the Left today. The *real* problem, I shall suggest, is both less complex and more brutal than it is commonly presented as being;
(3) the attempt to evict political economy totally from Marxism (which is what Thompson more or less attempts) actually weakens its explanatory force, and is also frequently accompanied by a moralistically anti-capitalist politics (see Chapter 3 above). However, since I have dealt with moralistic anti-capitalism already, I want to give most attention in this appendix to the theoretical issues surrounding point (2) above, whilst also touching briefly upon points (1) and (3).

The problem of 'reductionism' in Marxism

At one level, anybody who is familiar either with Marxist theory or with Marxist politics knows perfectly well what is meant by this term. It denotes the tendency to 'reduce' all propositions about culture, politics or group or individual consciousness to propositions about class position and/or economic self-interest. The most common forms are totally unwarranted universalizations of partial truths (e.g. 'the law is only a tool of the ruling class') and the drawing of dubious political conclusions from the partial truths so universalized (e.g. freedom of speech is a bourgeois freedom – broadly accurate as a historical generalization about origins – entails that it will have no place in a 'proletarian democracy' – false and horrifying conclusion). At its worst it simply degenerates into abuse (e.g. 'feminism is a petty-bourgeois deviation').

In the realm of politics and government, the problem is said to lie in Marxists treating all politics and all questions of government and the state as if they were merely economic or class questions in disguise. Thus when a Conservative minister announces that the privatization of medical care is being undertaken by the government in order 'to increase freedom of choice', reductionist Marxists say that this is not 'really' the reason this is being done, the 'real' reason is to provide the means by which the richer classes in society can have superior medical care. Here 'reductionism' means claiming a superior knowledge of the motives of others on the basis of a general model of the economy and society. But once again, it is fairly clear that as a theoretical problem this is hardly very serious. For we can rephrase the explanation in ways which do not require us to make any claim to superior knowledge of others' motivations. Thus we may say that the Conservative politician is motivated by the desire to 'increase freedom of choice', that the measure in question will have the consequence of increasing such freedom – for some people – but that it will also have the consequence of increasing the gap in the quality of health care available to the better-off against that available to the less well-off. Indeed, I think it can be shown that nearly all propositions in Marxism which refer to 'real' motivations (particularly those using 'false consciousness' ideas) can be re-expressed in terms of consequences (either actual or predicted) with the disappearance of many of the theoretical problems which inhere in 'motivation' formulations.

In fact, the very rehearsing of these examples shows that, at least in its crudest forms, what is termed *reductionism* has hardly any credence at all intellectually. Mostly it is a simple compound of historical ignorance and bad logic, and the fact that, for example, rhetorical abuse can itself have a marked political impact (that intelligent people will blanche and retreat when accused of having perpetrated a 'petty-bourgeois deviation' or taken up an 'anti-working class position') is a testimony to the curious psychological dynamics which are frequently operative in Marxist sects, but is hardly evidence of a serious intellectual problem.

In fact, 'reductionism' seems only to be a serious theoretical (as against political) problem in one specific context, the context of consciousness, and of the products of conscious thought and reflection (belief systems, cultural and artistic creations, symbolic constructions of all types). 'Reductionism' arises here when a cultural artifact (a novel, poem, painting) or a set of beliefs or perceptions either of an individual or a group are explained totally in terms either of the class position of their creator(s) or in terms of their economic self-interest. But, once again this theoretical position only has to be stated to make its absurdity manifest. I at least could not give a coherent account of what it might mean to 'explain totally' a novel or a poem or a legal system on the basis of class position or economic self-interest. It seems clear that both factors might enter in to specific explanations of specific aspects of novels, poems and legal systems. At the simpler end of the spectrum I might be able to relate the drafting and adjudication of property legislation to class interests or the keen interest of a novelist in the sales of his product to economic self-interest. To enter infinitely more subtle and complex issues, questions of social and natural perception, stresses and absences in a novel, and even certain aspects of style and imagery might be illuminated by a discussion of class-related sensibility, but that *all* of a legal system or *all* of the form and content of any cultural product could be explained purely in terms of class or economic self-interest is not merely a false notion, it is actually incoherent. What *could* be the class implications of the electric blue of the sky in Van Gogh's *Church at Auvers*?

I find myself irritated by making such obvious points, and

perhaps the reader will be too; but occasionally it is necessary to labour the obvious because in the heated exchange of emotionally loaded generalities (of which the debate about reductionism is a prime example), the obvious is often scorned by both sides with a consequent loss of clarity. Let me take this a little further into the realms of the even more irritatingly obvious. If I watch a children's television programme about cats and dogs and am told that this is 'bourgeois', does the reductionism here involved imply that the molecules and cells of the persons who make up the actual bourgeoisie (supposing them to be precisely identifiable) have been metamorphosed into scenery, sets, puppets wires and light waves? Obviously not. Assuming the allegation above to have any coherent meaning it refers to certain attitudes or values which the script or characterizations involved supposedly embody or demonstrate. But if this is what is meant, then the notion of 'reductionism' is simply inapposite. For there is no 'reductionism' here in the fairly precise sense that the term can be applied to, for example, 'reducing' propositions about brick walls to propositions about the atomic and sub-atomic particles of which the wall is composed. Propositions about plays, poems, novels, television programmes, legal systems or marriage customs cannot, in any strict sense, be 'reduced' to propositions about labour values, or rates of profit, or organic compositions of capital, because one is not talking about questions of scale in a one dimensional reality, but about different dimensions of a multi-dimensional reality. This is not to say that there are no relations among the different dimensions, but that the relations are not ones of scale or even (in any simple sense) of depth. In fact the spatial metaphor (of 'dimension') breaks down altogether when one tries to think about these relations in a more exact way.

Where then does the 'reductionist' metaphor come from? Very clearly it is simply another outcome of working with what I have elsewhere referred to as 'layer cake' or structuralist notions of social relations. Base and superstructure, scientific and ideological, social being and social consciousness, material and ideal — all these contrasts can be assimilated to a one-dimensional

hierarchical or 'cross-sectional' blueprint of social relations in
which the 'real determinate' (in the last instance of course) bits
are on the bottom holding the rest up ('the real foundation upon
which arises . . .'). Given this 'overdetermining' metaphor or
analogy, 'reductionism' fits in nicely. 'Reductionism' is one
solution to the problem of how you relate the top bits to the
bottom bits. It is the solution of saying that the top bits are 'really'
only the bottom bits in disguise, hence there are only bottom bits
really; everything is *reduced* to bottom bits. And this is exactly
why, when probed, 'reductionism' turns out to be a theoretically
incoherent notion. After all, nobody would ever say that because
the Eiffel Tower rests on foundations there are 'really' only the
foundations of the Eiffel Tower in existence.

Now Althusser tried, as Thompson noted, to get round this
problem by substituting for the layer-cake or static hierarchy
notion of these relations a machine analogy or metaphor. Here
the determinate, material, class relations are no longer conceived
of as foundations, but as prime movers in a mechanism. Once you
do this, however, it is even less clear how reductionism comes in,
since once again nobody would ever say that a clock was only
really a coiled spring. But in any case one is still fundamentally
misled in one's thinking by this analogy, because once again all
the parts of an engine or mechanism are the same kinds of thing
(inanimate materials of various types) and all exist in the same
dimension of space and time, and this clearly is not the case with
the various real and ideal phenomena which together constitute a
society or societies.

Now it is no news to anyone that analogies can mislead, but
since they seem to be indispensable to human thinking and
especially to the construction of abstract 'meta-languages', it is
well that we keep this in mind. Especially is it important that
Marxists keep it in mind, since in my view a very great deal of the
theoretical problems about reductionism derive from the fact that
whilst Marx and Engels were very good at actually doing
historical materialism, they were very sloppy constructors of a
Marxist meta-language about historical materialism. Engels in

particular, after Marx's death, threw around a lot of inapposite and muddled analogies and metaphors, acceptable perhaps as crude gestures in vague directions but utterly pernicious if hammered into structuralist tablets of stone. There is no better – or rather worse – example of this than the utterly arid and formalistic debate which emerged after Althusser's structuralist treatment of 'determination in the last instance'.

So if the traditional base/superstructure analogy is misleading or worse and leads to the false problem of 'reductionism', how can we do better? Perhaps by having recourse to an analogy from natural science.

Supposing we have a piece of wood of which we have two descriptions. One is by the proverbial person from the top of the Clapham omnibus and the other is by an atomic physicist. The first description contains a measurement of length, breadth and depth, notes the colour of the wood and the presence of two knots in the surface and some splinters where it has been roughly sawn at one end. The atomic physicist, however, provides a chart of the wood's molecular structure and some formulae to describe its atomic and sub-atomic composition. Which of these descriptions is the 'true' description of the piece of wood? The interesting thing about this question is that it appears to have no im- mediately obvious answer. We cannot simply say that one description is true and the other false. We want to say that both are true. Thinking further we might want to say that the physicist's description is at a 'deeper level of reality' than that of the Clapham bus passenger, and indeed some theories of science (which see atoms and sub-atomic particles as just very small bits of things) would endorse this notion of a 'deeper level' as being very precise. But even so, one would not be justified in saying that the physicist's description was in any simply sense 'better' or 'superior' to the ordinary person's, because it was at a 'deeper level'. It is certainly in a positivistic (non-normative) sense a more 'scientific' description (since atomic physics as an activity is classed as a science but ordinary perception is not), but this does not make it 'better'. Indeed 'better' or 'worse' here can have no meaning apart from questions of utility. If you were thinking of using the piece of wood to make a cabinet, then the ordinary person's description would certainly be better since it would save you doing the measuring and you could allow for the knots. If, on the other hand, one needed some data for an examination in atomic physics . . .

I believe that there are limited but important parallels to be drawn between this case and the case of economic and non-economic descriptions and explanations in historical material-ism. Everything turns on the use to which economic and non-economic descriptions and explanations are being put, and debates about the explanatory force or merit of different types of explanation which abstract from the question of the uses of explanation are doomed to end in frustration and mutual incomprehension. This confusion is worse confounded when questions of causality are brought in.

In analyzing these issues I shall be concerned with the relationship between explanations of 'underlying' economic relations of capitalism and forms of class consciousness, since this is a central political and theoretical preoccupation of Thompson's. This is not the only issue which might be dealt with, since Marxism also contains a central body of propositions about changes in modes of production (feudalism to capitalism, capitalism to socialism and communism) and the changes in juridical, political and cultural relations and in human conscious-ness which these are supposed or predicted to bring in their train. Neglect of this issue does not indicate that I think it unimportant or unproblematic but simply reflects the fact that Thompson has had far less to say about it, perhaps because by definition these kinds of total system changes have been rare in history, and the practising historian of capitalism, and indeed the socialist living in a capitalist society is primarily concerned with analytical issues within this one mode of production. However, the way one understands the formation and reproduction of human con-sciousness under capitalism profoundly affects, as Thompson himself has brilliantly demonstrated, the way one will conceive of revolution and socialist construction.

In what follows then I lay out what I take to be the essence of Marx's political economy and suggest how it may be understood and used in non- 'economistic' or 'reductionist' ways.

Marx's *Capital* is, among other things, a highly sophisticated dynamic model of the way in which industrial output is divided between a 'class' of direct producers and a 'class' of owners of the means of production. Given a certain institutional structure (basically private property on the one hand and a property-less proletariat on the other), the fundamental division of output is between profit (going to the owners of means of production) and wages (going to the proletariat). A number of variables are then derived which affect this division (i.e. may alter it over time). These are:

(1) the rate of capital accumulation (determined by saving and investment from profits accumulated by the class of 'capitalists');
(2) the size and structure of the reserve army of labour. This has an important influence on the share of output going to wages, and is itself determined by both the rate of population growth and the rate and type of capital accumulation (especially the substitution of capital for labour).

However, at the heart of the model and lying behind both these variables is the concept of the *productivity of labour*. Marx's central insight, the insight which took him beyond Ricardo, was that if capital was accumulated so fast that the supply of 'excess' labour from peasant agriculture and from population growth to industry was exhausted (so that there is something approaching full employment), then the class of capitalists can only prevent the share of wages in output rising (eating into profits) by increasing the productivity of the labour expended. This is done largely by enhancing human energy and skill with ever greater and more sophisticated amounts of machinery. In particular, the crucial relationship is between (1) the mass of commodities consumed by the class of direct producers as their 'subsistence', and (2) the productivity of the labourers producing these commodities ('wage goods'). If the former rises faster than the latter, then the share of wages in total output rises and profits fall. If the latter rises faster than the former then the share of wages in output falls and profits rise. Given a total magnitude ('output'), its division into two ('profits' and 'wages') and the analytical specification of two classes of people whose income comes entirely and exclusively from one or other of these sources, then clearly one has a zero-sum game. If one 'class' gains the other must (where 'must' means 'must logically') lose. Subsidiary parts of the model then specify the motives which the class of capitalists have for replacing or supplementing living labour with 'dead labour' (machinery). These are (1) competition between capitalists, and (2) the tendency of capital accumulation to expand faster than the reserve army. On the workers' side it is assumed that the desire to be materially better off is sufficient motive for attempts to increase wages. Marx did not consider the effect of trade unions, though if he had done it would only have strengthened the force of the basic dynamic which he posits. Note also, of course, that the supplementation of living labour with machinery tends to increase continuously the amount of output as well as continually lowering its unit cost in labour time expended (its 'value'). If output rises fast enough, then even if the respective shares of profits and wages remain stable (i.e. there is stalemate in the economic 'class struggle') everybody can be absolutely better off over time. Recognition of this fact has for a long time made social democrats keen advocates of economic growth.

Now for the purposes of the present discussion two points need to be noted. At this level of abstraction the concept of 'class' is a purely analytical one. Marx is here talking of classes of people in the way that philosophers talk about 'predicative classes' ('there is a class of object such that . . . all toys are red, or all balls are blue'). For this model to work there is simply no necessity for the 'classes' of capitalists or workers so specified to have any common consciousness, any shared culture or values. All that the model requires is that individual capitalists firms should desire their profits to rise, or at least not to fall, and that individual workers should desire to raise their real wages or (what in this context amounts to the same thing) their standard of living. It says that if these conditions are met then there must be a constant class struggle (in this very narrow economic sense) over the division of total output. Now we know that as a matter of historical fact these conditions were met and that they still are met, and given the other conditions specified by the model (capitalist firms competing in a free market situation and a class of direct producers totally dependent upon wages to live) this is scarcely surprising. Of course it is an historical question as to how these necessary preconditions came about (how a class of industrial capitalists and a proletariat was formed) and Marx has something to say about both questions, though more about the latter than the former. But the point is that once they exist the class struggle must commence and it will continue as long as they exist and the actors in the situation act as the model specifies.

It is notable also that the model works with two sets of categories, some which are clearly known to the actors in the situation and others which may not be. Thus, both capitalists and workers are aware of (i.e. can perceive empirically) what is happening to their profits and wages respectively and are deemed to respond in various ways to rises or falls in these magnitudes. But for the model to work it is not necessary for either workers or capitalists to be aware of what (on a global level) is happening to the share of profits and wages in total output. Changes in these shares are an effect of activity which need not be motivated by a conscious awareness of either 'total output' or the 'share of profit' or the 'share of wages'. Indeed it is assumed that neither individual capitalists or groups of capitalists, nor individual workers or groups of workers are concerned with these global magnitudes. They are concerned purely with their (individual) profits and their (individual) wages at any particular moment in time. However, whether this is so, or whether as an historical assumption it is out of date (i.e. there are government 'think tanks' and trade union research departments monitoring these macro-level shares) the crucial point is that it is changes in these shares that 'really matter' for the capitalist system. Why is this? Quite simply because if the share of profits falls below the level necessary to sustain capital accumulation and continued increases in productivity, then the real standards of living of both workers and capitalists will fall. Most obviously they will fall relative to other capitalist systems which are maintaining higher rates of accumulation, but if the share of profit drops far enough, they will begin to fall in absolute terms. Now note that this is all that one can say on the basis of the model alone. There is no warrant whatsoever for supposing that if they fall there will be revolution, or fascism, or socialism, or conservatism or social democracy, nor for supposing that if the share of profits and the rate of accumulation remains stable or rises there will be social consensus, or political stability, or revolt against materialism, or an ecological crisis, or fascism, or socialism, or conservatism, or social democracy. What there will be will be determined by a much broader historical process embracing a mass of variables unknown to the model. As a matter of fact, we know that even comparatively small falls in general living standards, especially if they are very unequally distributed, do usually result in increased social tensions of various sorts, and if the falls are large and sudden the tensions are commensurately greater. But one cannot go beyond this broad but not totally vacuous formulation unless one 'does history'. Because without empirical work there is simply no way of making it more precise, i.e. at this point analysis would have to concern itself specifically with post-1815 England and France, or Weimar Germany, or Britain in the late seventies and eighties.

In short, Marx's basic political economy tells us only a narrow truth, but the truth is not the less important for being so narrow. The concentration upon the division of total output between wages and profits and the closely related issue of capital accumulation and labour productivity reveal:

(a) the necessary (but not sufficient) conditions for capitalism remaining a dynamic and materially prosperous system (delivering the goods, literally), and

(b) an invariant concomitant of declines in its dynamism and material prosperity.

Now that really isn't bad, even if it doesn't quite add up to the total 'laws of motion' for which the Old Man was looking. It especially isn't bad considering that at the time he only had one semi-fledged empirical case out of which to abstract his essential model.

To return, however, to the question of consciousness. Will workers go on strike, and if so how will they feel about it when they do? Will they join political organizations and if so which ones and why? Will all workers (wage workers, whether direct producers or not) see their employment situation in the same way, and if not, why not? Will the experience of work be the same for men and women and if not, why not? Will all capitalists be equally nice or equally nasty, will they think of themselves as 'capitalists' at all (will all the workers think of themselves as 'workers'?)? How will artisans and shopkeepers and civil servants and painters and poets and writers think and feel about capitalism and other things? On the basis of the model we don't know and we can't know (which is not to say that Marx did not make comments and observations on some of these things in *Capital* and elsewhere). If we want to find out, then we must do what he did, which is to engage in empirical work.

This is not to say, however, that one cannot extrapolate from the model in order to try and arrive at answers, but the problem is that unless such extrapolation is very carefully disciplined by empirical work, it is likely to turn into wishful thinking and false prediction (as it did in *Capital*). For example, Marx opined that men and women sharing the common experience of industrial wage slavery would rapidly develop a consciousness of shared oppression on which a socialist or at least revolutionary consciousness would arise. Now the first extrapolation (from wage slavery to common consciousness) has been shown to be at best a partial truth, much affected and qualified by other factors, and the second (from common consciousness to revolutionary consciousness) has been proved largely false. This is not to deny that such extrapolations might have seemed warranted in Britain in the 1850s, but as a matter of historical fact we do know them to have been too easy.

Marx is always attempting this kind of extrapolation from his model in *Capital* (he plays with yet others in the *Grundrisse*), but the harsh truth is that there is no way of getting from the kernel of the model, purely deductively, to any determinate conclusion about the prospects for revolutionary class consciousness or socialism or anything else. There are a large number of alternative possible trajectories for any society of which capitalism forms the economic core and out of this range of possibilities the actual historical ones are determined by a host of factors (including the actual beliefs and values of men and women) whose combination is not purely deducible. Deduction must be combined with induction (the dialectical method) which is also good history and good theory. But nonetheless the kernel remains. It acts as a broad constraint upon capitalism, so long as it is capitalism, and it ensures the existence of an always continuing economic class struggle, which may, however, co-exist either with total or near total ideological consensus or with violent revolution or with any intermediate state.

One further related point about 'exploitation' and Marx's basic model, a point which is central to Thompson's own work: in our ABCs of Marxism we all learn that Marx saw capital accumulation as occurring out of exploitation 'at the point of production'. Workers work for a certain length of time and produce a certain amount of commodities which they then use to reproduce themselves (wage goods). They then continue to work (or more exactly are constrained so to do) and produce an excess or surplus, which the capitalist accumulates as profit. When measured or enumerated in labour time units the commodities which make up the wage bundle are called the 'variable capital', the excess or surplus is the 'surplus value' or surplus labour time units. We thus get to the famous $\frac{s}{v}$ which Marx tells us is 'the rate of surplus value or the rate of exploitation'. Now there is no doubt that in *any* capitalist economy there is a rate of surplus value, i.e. a ratio of surplus output to wage goods output. It is in that sense a purely technical macro-economic concept. But in hooking this up to the concept of 'exploitation' with all its other connotations (of nastiness, misery, suffering, the grinding of faces), Marx was both pulling off a political and propaganda coup and making a conflation which, however understandable at the time, has rather peculiar results if applied to contemporary capitalism. The complications arise moreover because of the importance both contemporaneously and in the historical development of capitalism of what Marx in his basic model termed 'relative surplus value', i.e. raising the mass and rate of surplus value not by lengthening the working day ('absolute' surplus value) but by increasing the productivity of each unit of labour time by the addition of ever greater and more productive amounts of machinery. The net result of this in 1983 is that if a worker is earning £200 per week, but his or her output is £800 per week, we must, on Marx's model, consider him or her more exploited than a worker earning £80 per week, but whose output is only £160 per week, for in the latter case the rate of surplus value is 100 per cent, whereas in the former case it is 400 per cent.

Now such a notion is not entirely without significance for it directs our attention to a very important truth about the industrial working class under contemporary capitalism, viz. that its most prosperous sections are usually also its most productive sections, i.e. those whose labour yields most surplus per unit of labour time (and this is true both nationally and internationally). It also restresses a familiar theme in *Capital*, which is that the worker is only employed so long as his or her labour is productive for the capitalist and that he or she has no choice but to work for the benefit of another.

Nonetheless the proposition that a worker paid £200 per week is 'more exploited' than one earning around the current industrial minimum wage is one that most working people (and indeed most people) would find puzzling if not ridiculous. And this is because the term 'exploitation' still maintains all the very negative and emotional connotations which Marx was quite consciously trying to conscript to his side when he equated the rate of surplus value with the 'rate of exploitation'. So long as workers whose labour yielded surplus value were also workers earning subsistence wages, working in appalling conditions and returning home in rags to hovels (or even so long as the majority of workers approximated these conditions) such an equation carried a certain conviction. Politically too it was possible to combine loosely analytical terms like 'wage slavery' and 'surplus value' to the rhetoric of 'exploitation' and to have no doubts that the latter at least would strike an echo in the day-to-day experience of working people. It is possible that it still does so, but in the Britain of today the experience of exploitation for the majority of working people has much more to do with the monotony of work, management attitudes, or perhaps simply with being constrained to pass one's day in ways one would not have chosen than it will have to do with the more naked experience of absolute poverty and degradation.

In short then, there is a fascinating conflation of the technical (the scientific?) and the experiential in Marx's concept of exploitation, a conflation which was at one time perhaps a political strength but which the development of capitalism itself has now rendered a weakness (a weakness painfully enacted day after day in trying to sell the *Socialist Worker* or the *Morning Star* to the 'proletariat' at the factory gate as they hurry to their Cortinas). But this conflation/ambiguity is a rich theme in the real history of the British (and French and German and American) working class as well as in the history of Marxism itself.

Through it one could examine such issues as the claims of Marxism to be 'scientific', the relationship between Marxist theory and Marxist politics and the relationship between changing material circumstances and changing class consciousness in real, individual capitalist societies. But – and this is the point – a very great deal of that richness is lost if one simply removes that ambiguity by adopting a concept of exploitation which focuses exclusively on the way in which proletarianization was experienced by workers, and this, as Richard Johnson* quite

---

* Richard Johnson, 'Edward Thompson, Eugene Genovese and Socialist-Humanist History', *History Workshop Journal*, no. 6, Autumn 1978, pp. 79–100.

correctly argued, is precisely what Thompson did in *The Making of the English Working Class*. And the reason for his persistent tendency to collapse exploitation into the experience of exploitation (which Johnson brings out so well in his analysis of some crucial passages in the book) is, I think, Thompson's conviction – which may not be entirely intellectual – that the use of any explanation of human behaviour which posits determinants outside the consciousness of the people being explained is potentially, if not actually, Stalinist. It is potentially Stalinist because from such explanations one may move to posit that the workers, like the Marxist theorist, ought to see the 'objective truth' of their situation. If they do not it is because they suffer from 'false consciousness', and if they suffer from 'false consciousness' then they can only be liberated by an élite with the science to guarantee 'true consciousness', and hence on down a familiar trail. Since Thompson will, rightly, have none of this, he wants to cut the disease at its root which is this form of explanation or analysis itself. But again, if one looks back over the last sentence, the passage from the initial analytical position to the Stalinist consequences is made up of a series of logical leaps, all of which involve choosing one among a number of very different political implications which are logically open to one. In short, it is perfectly possible to hold to the initial analytical position without accepting any of its Stalinist implications. One way of doing so (and here we return by a vastly circuitous route to the wood splinters and the atoms) is simply to say that there is no incompatibility between the proposition that a worker is the source of a large amount of surplus for capital (and that he or she is in that sense highly exploited) and the worker's conviction that he or she has never been better off, works for a very good employer, and is not in the least exploited. There is no meaningful sense in which the latter proposition (and thus the consciousness in which it is embodied) can be regarded as 'false' because the former proposition is 'true'. It all depends on the use to which the propositions are being put. In the first case the Marxist theorist is endeavouring to explain why an employer seeking to maximize his or its (it is more likely to be a corporation these days) profits should find it worthwhile to pay workers high wages, and indeed why it should be able to do so. In the second case the worker is endeavouring to make implicit historical comparisons with his or her own previous work and living situation, and/or with those of his or her parents. Since this has improved, is improving, and is expected, not totally irrationally, to go on improving, the denial of exploitation is in this context perfectly 'true'. The most that one could perhaps say is that the latter proposition is true at the level of appearances, while the former is a more essential truth about capitalism. Here, carrying forward some ideas derived from Marx's famous chapter on fetishism of commodities in Capital, one says that the underlying dynamics of capitalism throw up a realm of appearances which is yet not an imaginary or unreal realm, but simply the appearance that the underlying reality assumes, as wood atoms appear (quite 'correctly') as knots, colour and splinters. However, even if one does take this position, there can be no warrant for moving from that to any élitist political position. The knowledge of 'essence' is no 'better' than the knowledge of 'appearance' in any unqualified sense. In particular, if the majority of workers do not experience exploitation, then knowledge of the essence and indeed attempts to communicate it to the workers, will get nowhere. It will simply be regarded as false knowledge (which from their point of view it certainly is). It will have no political efficacy whatsoever.

This section of the appendix has been especially addressed to Thompson's arguments in The Poverty of Theory about the role of political economy in Marx's Capital as well as to his broader preoccupations with Stalinism. I consider the section on Capital and classical political economy in the book to be its weakest part, not simply because I disagree with it but because it seems to me to be woefully, and very untypically, misinformed.

Thus, Thompson says of Capital that 'As pure political economy it may be faulted for introducing external categories; its laws cannot be verified, and its predictions were wrong'. However:

(1) Though some of Marx's predictions were wrong (the immiserization thesis [on some readings], and the 'law' of the declining rate of profits), others were right (the increasing concentration and centralization of capital, capitalism's continued capacity to revolutionize the forces and relations of production).

(2) Much more interestingly, one can use Marx's basic model of capitalism to criticize and reveal the flawed logic on which his more rash predictions were based. The most interesting case here is the 'law' of the falling rate of profit, which can be shown to be formally inconsistent with the demands of raising relative surplus value.

(3) Although all of Marx's basic economic concepts are formulated in value terms and it is notorious that in the real world values cannot be measured (they also pose theoretical problems in cases like 'joint production' of two or more commodites by one production process), they may still maintain their validity in other respects (principally as a means of drawing attention to the real social relations which underly the accumulation of capital) and can be perfectly adequately replaced by other empirically measurable magnitudes (for example, the share of wages and the share of profits) when measurement is required.

In short, the whole issue is a lot more complex than Thompson appears to suppose, so complex in fact as to have engaged some of the best young economic theorists in Britain, Japan and Italy for the last ten or so years, without some questions being satisfactorily resolved – a measure of the difficulty of the issues with which Marx was dealing. It is clear that Thompson is either ignorant of, or perhaps simply not interested in, Marx's economic theory, and here at the risk of seeming both arrogant and condescending I must enter some speculations about Thompson's Marxism, and indeed about the Marxism of the whole group of young Communist Party historians and social scientists of which he was a distinguished member.

I think it is true to say that if one was learning one's Marxism in the forties or early fifties and especially if one was reading *Capital*

162 / Rethinking Socialism

at that time, one was working in a general intellectual ambiance in which, even on the Left, Marx's reputation as an economic theorist was at a very low ebb. He could still be highly regarded, in conventional terms, as an historian, a sociologist of industry and 'class', even as a philosopher and political theorist, but as an economist, went the conventional wisdom, he was *passé*. A few diehards like Maurice Dobb, Paul Sweezy and Ronald Meek were continuing to put up a valiant rearguard action in his defence, but for the most part neo-classical economics ruled. Everybody knew that the labour theory of value had been 'disproved' or 'superseded'; and even if one read Marx sympathetically, one read him for the history, for the brilliant strokes of synthesizing insight and genius, or just for the polemic – but not for the economics. Now, if in addition one's personal intellectual predilections were not in that direction, it must have been quite a relief to pass over all that dreary stuff about 'commodities' and 'values' and 'exchange' and get on to the history.

But it must be said, quite unequivocally, that this view was wrong. Marx is an economic theorist of immense distinction and power, and a great deal of the history of economic theory over the last twenty or so years has been the rediscovery of that fact. Especially in the wake of Piero Sraffa, it has been widely concluded that Marx (and indeed Ricardo and the classical school in general) had answers to some of the fundamental questions of economic theory which are at least as good, and in certain areas a good deal better (more logically consistent) than the answers provided by neo-classical economics. To be sure, the new interest in Marx (in obscure things like 'the transformation problem' and in values as a mode of enumerating production which Dobb and the other old hands used to go on about in difficult tracts) has not left Marx's theory unchanged, nor suggested that it was right in every respect. But it has deepened and widened our understanding of the issues with which he was trying to grapple and the brilliance of the attempt which he made. A great deal of this new work upon Marxist economics was done by young economists in Britain connected with the Conference of

Socialist Economists, in the 1970s. Moreover, most of the gifted contributors to that new research and debate on Marx's value theory (Steadman, Rowthorn, Hodgson, Glyn, Armstrong, Harrison, Elson) are all notable precisely for their lack of 'economism' and 'reductionism'. It is clear that Thompson had not read this work when he wrote *The Poverty of Theory*, for if he had, some of the more easy generalizations about the 'post-Stalinist generation' would not have slipped so easily from his pen.

In short, I think that Richard Johnson hit the nail squarely on the head when he noted the marked gap between Maurice Dobb and the later generation of Communist historians of whom Thompson was one, and I think it unfortunate that he should have detracted from the force of this point by muddying the water with, for the most part, inapposite generalities about structuralism. British Marxism (if that is a meaningful conception) lost its way rather badly when it lost that combination of sophisticated command over economic theory and deep interest in history which so distinguished Maurice Dobb. What took its place was a history denuded, not of theory in its entirety, but of some crucial explanatory tools.

I want now to summarize the argument of this section. I have suggested that:

(1) 'reductionism' and 'economism', whilst serious political problems within Marxism, are not serious theoretical problems. By this I mean that they derive from a particular methodological image or analogy for historical materialism (what I term the 'layer cake' analogy) for which Marx and especially Engels must accept some responsibility, but which when closely examined turns out to be totally inapposite. It is an example of very imperfect or sloppy 'meta-language' from which Marxism has certainly suffered. When the analogy is exploded, then 'reductionism' as a serious theoretical problem largely disappears as well. It turns out to be as incoherent a theoretical notion as the broader notion by which it is overdetermined. This does not mean that the political problem of reductionism (as a way of thinking and arguing) disappears, but it does mean that:

(2) it is possible to reassert the worth and power of certain economic formulations and explanations in Marxism (what may broadly be termed Marx's 'basic political economy') without that necessarily leading one to 'economism'. I have tried to demonstrate that Marx's political economy is capable of generating a small number of important but quite narrow propositions even about contemporary capitalism, which however carry no necessary (i.e. logically necessary) political consequences, or consciousness consequences. The most important propositions concern:

(a) *the essential prerequisites of economic growth under capitalism* and (the converse of this) the essential mechanisms of its decline or 'crisis' as a materially productive system, and

(b) *the 'objective' character of exploitation under capitalism.* The latter notion, however, is seen to be connotatively ambiguous, and it is suggested that an exploration of that ambiguity is an important theme both in actual working-class social and political history and in the history of Marxism as a body of thought and as a political practice. I have argued that Thompson's loss of that ambiguity (by the collapse of exploitation totally into the experience of exploitation) is one of the central weaknesses of his major historical work.

The section ended by some speculations about the formation of Thompson's Marxism and in particular about the effective absence of economic theory from his Marxism. It was suggested that the revolt against 'economism' (which was for Thompson one of the crucial lessons of 1956) may also have gelled well both with personal intellectual predilections and with the contemporary conventional wisdom about Marx's status as an economist. This conventional wisdom was, however, just wrong, and more recent work in economic theory has shown it to be so. An appreciation of that work leads to, among other things, a realization of how limited a role economic explanations *per se* can play in Marxism. In short, the best young Marxist economists are very rarely 'economistic'. The sort of 'economism' which

'Messrs Hindess and Hirst' manifested in their early work (but not now) is much more a trait of those who, unsteady in their command of Marx's basic political economy, are, for that reason as much as any other, predisposed to think that it is capable of explaining and predicting far more than it can do. However, that this predisposition has been such a persistant one in Marxism is scarcely surprising given the tendency even of the Old Man himself to extrapolate from his basic model in ways which were far from logically watertight and sometimes owed more to wishful thinking than empirical evidence.

The real problem of Stalinism

So far I have argued that the obsession not only of Edward Thompson but of a great deal of western Marxism with exorcizing economic 'reductionism' is, in theoretical terms, largely misconceived. A commitment to some of the central concepts of Marx's political economy need not necessarily lead to the adoption of élitist or Stalinist political positions, and in any case, in a strict philosophical sense the notion of 'reducing' all non-economic phenomena in society to economic or class terms is actually incoherent.

However, this does not mean that Stalinism is not a serious problem in Marxism. I will argue, however, that it is at once a much simpler and more deeply rooted problem than it appears in much abstract debate about 'economism', 'determinism', etc. 'Stalinism' comprises a number of specific events and trends in the history of Marxism which can be simply described, were and are disastrous and ugly in their consequences, and certainly need to be discussed. However, one does not need to be a philosopher of social science (either real or *manqué*) to discuss them. In fact they emerge far more clearly and appallingly if they are not befuddled by confused debates about the nature of historical or sociological method. Three of these problems are particularly important.

(1) In situations where Marxists take power in materially poor

166 / Rethinking Socialism

and underdeveloped countries, the view that socialism and the
'realm of freedom' require, as a necessary condition, a considerable growth of the 'forces of production' can lead one to the
view that there can be no freedom (at least for the majority) until
that (vaguely specified) stage is reached. Hence Stalin's labour
camps, enforced collectivization, denial of the right to strike (and
indeed most other rights) to peasants and industrial workers. In
short, the sacrifice of all other objectives to that of maximizing
economic growth under state control entails dictatorship, even
totalitarianism. It seems to me that when many socialists
(including E.P. Thompson) worry about 'economism' this is at
least a part, perhaps the major part, of what they are actually
worrying about – not abstruse questions about what one makes
of worker consciousness or activity if one holds to the theory of
surplus value.

(2) There is a version of the 'consequences' solution to the
problem of motivation or consciousness (see page 145 above)
which can be particularly horrifying. This is the view that says 'if
the consequence of A's action is B, then he "objectively" intended
B, even if "subjectively" he did not'. Hence in the class struggle,
consequences *are* intentions. To be more precise, if the desire of
Germany is to damage the economy of the USSR and the
consequences of the policies advocated and pursued by Nikolai
Bukharin damage the economy of the USSR, then Nikolai
Bukharin is 'objectively' a German agent, though he may not be
'subjectively' (criterion of guilt in Stalin's show trials).

(3) If one is living in a western democratic country and one holds
that the liberties and freedoms existing in that country (of the
press, of speech, of assembly, of freedom from arbitrary arrest)
are 'bourgeois' freedoms (i.e. freedoms won historically by the
bourgeoisie in opposition to absolutist states), then as we have
already noted, one can imply that in a socialist state where the
proletariat – not the bourgeoisie – is the ruling class, there will be
no place or need for such freedoms.

Now clearly it is possible to treat all these three as 'theoretical'
problems, i.e. as problems in Marxist theory. If one does so, they

can be made to disappear fairly rapidly. I have already suggested that (3) rests on bad logic. It must be obvious that (2) also does so. Clearly the view that the consequences of the actions of an individual or group require an assessment separate from that of their intentions does not entail that consequences are intentions, or that intentions don't matter in making moral or legal judgements upon the consequences. Similarly, in the case of problem (1) one may argue either that:

(a) this is simply not a problem for Marxists lucky enough to be living in relatively prosperous societies already possessed of some meaningful degree of political freedom and democracy, or that

(b) in any case there were ways of obtaining a rapid growth of the forces of production and material prosperity in the USSR that would not have required anything like the same price in human freedom as was involved in the Stalinist strategy. In 'theoretical' terms this is just another way of saying that Stalin's logic was bad; the means to the end that he employed were not the only efficacious means available to that end, as he thought.

Clearly (b) above is a much more difficult argument to make than (a) because it involves the interpretation of historical evidence, and as everyone knows, there was and is fierce debate around such interpretation. But in any event, to take these quite precise political and historical problems and issues, appalling both in their reality and in their moral implications, and to transmogrify them into 'theoretical' problems of 'economism', 'reductionism', etc. – to treat them abstractly as epistemological problems of theory and method (so that they apply at least potentially as much to discussions of the English Civil War, the Peasants' Revolt, or the French Revolution as to Stalinist labour camps) – is a highly idealist procedure. It is in fact to fail to engage with these specific historical and political problems (Stalin's show trials, collectivization, the Comintern's 'social fascist' period) by seeing them idealistically as somehow 'entailed' in the discourse of Volume I of *Capital*. It is in a curious way to specify the problem wrongly, to abstract and universalize it in a way that leads to highly confused intellectual debate and at the same time allows one to fudge the real problem. By engaging with everything one in fact engages with nothing.

But surely, it will be contended, one cannot make such a total distinction between Marxist ideas and the uses to which they are put? Surely the ideas about Marxism that Stalin carried in his head are not entirely irrelevant to his actions as a dictator? And this must also be true of Lenin's behaviour, of the actions of the German Social Democratic Party or of the Mensheviks? Certainly no historical analyses of these phenomena can be utterly abstracted from the influences of ideas. But in all these cases the precise issue is the way in which Marxist ideas were appropriated by the people in question, and the issue of appropriation is a much more complex one than can be grasped by mere textual exegesis of *Capital*, the *Communist Manifesto* or whatever. It involves the subtle interrelationship between circumstances – the problems with which people like Lenin and Stalin were confronted at specific moments – and their selection from the considerable corpus of Marxist thought, of those ideas to which they would give prominence at those moments. In addition however, their very identity as Marxists influenced the way in which Lenin and Stalin perceived the 'circumstances' and 'problems', so there is a familiar dialectic here between ideas and material reality. However, to jump immediately from specific historical conjunctures to Marx's work – to ask, in effect, what it was in *Capital* that caused Stalin to hold show trials or put millions of people into labour camps (which is very much Professor Popper's procedure, for example) is precisely to fail to engage with this complex and historically specific problem of the *appropriation* of ideas.

In short, Stalin (or Lenin, Kautsky, Rosa Luxemburg or Mao) may be shown to be guilty of faulty logic, or of this or that 'crudity' of conceptualization, but in themselves such demonstrations do not tell us why. If Stalin believed that all forms of democracy had to be suppressed in an effort to 'build the productive forces', if Lenin and Trotsky came near to such beliefs at specific moments in the 1920s, if specific aspects of SPD strategy in Germany were influenced by its leadership's belief in the 'inevitability' of socialism, then to explain why these things were believed one has to do far more than seek for logical or philosophical weaknesses in Marx's classical texts. One has to engage with the full complexity of specific moments in the history of the USSR and Germany, of which Marxist ideas were merely a part. One does not make political and historical problems and crimes disappear theoretically, nor do I even think one guards effectively against such things happening again by 'correcting' such 'deviations' theoretically. On the contrary, one guards most effectively against the repetition of history by understanding history and by acting differently in the future, not by theoretical refinement.

This does not mean that I think the corpus of Marx's own ideas to be perfect, or free from responsibility from what was later done in his name. On the contrary, I think that, as has often been suggested (most recently and brilliantly by Kolakowski)*, Marx fudged some absolutely crucial issues about the construction of socialism and communism because of his essentially philosophical understanding of them as the transcendance or annulment of human alienation under capitalism. Thus, for Marx, the essence of the revolution against capitalism was the reappropriation of human products ('commodities') from their alienated state as commodities to the directly controlled and comprehended product of human beings (albeit now specified in class terms – 'the proletariat'). As a result, Marx never confronted the problem of creating actual institutions in real societies by which such a total 'unalienated' control of the environment could be, at the same time, meaningfully democratic. Or at the very least, his confrontation of this problem was woefully inadequate and question-begging. He seemed to suppose that an advanced and

---

* Leszek Kolakowski, *Main Currents of Marxism*: vol. 1, *The Founders*, Oxford, Oxford University Press, 1978.

complex industrial society could be run by very small-scale self-governing communes of workers (*à la* the Paris Commune) in what was essentially an anarchist vision of the state. The very real problems of socialist construction in the real world (of bureaucracy, of democratic control of a vastly expanded state, of efficiency in the use of natural and human resources, above all of how one concentrates and centralizes economic and social power without the emergence of despotism) were thus simply conjured away or left to solution by 'revolutionary praxis'. Thus these problems had to be confronted in reality in a totally *ad hoc* way, by the Bolsheviks, operating not, as had been supposed, in an advanced capitalist society but in a poor and backward one, and in the desperate circumstances of war, civil war, collapse of industry and infrastructure. Moreover, these enormously damaging *lacunae* in Marx's thought concerning the construction of socialism and its relationship to democracy and freedom were exacerbated by his underestimation of the significance and importance of bourgeois democratic freedoms and political institutions. The underestimation derived from his living in an epoch when absolutist government was still the predominant political form in mainland Europe, and in a Britain in which parliamentary democracy was still, fairly unambiguously, a form of rule by coalition of the bourgeoisie and aristocracy (consequent upon a very narrow franchise). It is true that Marx and Engels themselves probably did believe that some of the 'bourgeois' freedoms (of speech, of assembly, of political and religious belief, etc.) should have an important role in a socialist society too. But their ambiguity about this in their writings and above all their conviction that under capitalism these freedoms were only substantively available to the bourgeoisie although formally available universally, left plenty of room for totally different interpretations by later Marxists. Once again, however, as the above account I hope suggests, one can only come to terms with these weaknesses in classical Marxism by treating the work of Marx and Engels as a specific historical phenomenon and not as some timeless corpus of 'theory' which can only be 'correctly' or 'incorrectly' grasped.

Such an historical perspective allows one to see changes in the theoretical positions and emphases of Marx and Engels (whether upon capitalism or upon socialism and communism) as a response to changing historical and political situations. It also allows one to see the theoretical and political ambiguities in classical Marxism as a part (perhaps even an inevitable part) of its nature as an historical product, and therefore as something much more profound and intractable than mere 'theoretical' weaknesses. These ambiguities were created in and part of political practice and can therefore only be overcome by later generations of Marxists and socialists in and through such practice. It follows from this that it is in the actual creation of a democratic socialist politics and in the creation by democratic means of free socialist societies that the 'theoretical' problems of Marxism will be truly solved.

I think that actual 'workers', actual 'proletarians' in the real world would be a lot more impressed by such an achievement than by a library full of theoretical solutions (no matter how 'correct'), and quite rightly too. Any number of demonstrations that, in theory, socialism and freedom are not necessarily opposed will fail to cut much ice so long as the bulk of societies which are self-consciously socialist are very unfree societies, and so long as all societies that have any meaningful degree of political freedom and democracy are capitalist societies. As long as this is the case, it will be widely suspected that there must be something wrong with a theory that has so regularly produced dictatorships when attempts have been made to apply it in practice. I have already suggested some respects in which I think that such suspicions are correct, and how it might be possible to obtain better results in future by making substantial changes/ additions to the theory (pp. 29–47). But the crucial test has always to be a practical one, a political one, showing that socialism and freedom can be combined by actually combining them in reality.

To summarize the argument to this point, I have suggested that the coupling of socialism and freedom that has been assumed in this book is precisely what is contested both in the attacks of non-

Marxists upon Marxism (Karl Popper's *The Open Society and its Enemies* is still probably the best known of these attacks) and in some debates within Marxism. In the latter case, E.P. Thompson's *The Poverty of Theory* is a powerful restatement of a socialist humanist critique of the 'reductionism' and 'economic determinism' in classical Marxism, and what he sees as its renaissance in the work of Louis Althusser and his disciples (the latter seeming, at times, to include all of the English New Left!). In so far as 'economism', 'reductionism' and 'determinism' are presented as abstract philosophical or theoretical characteristics necessarily present in Marxism (which is how both Popper and Thompson, albeit in very different ways, present them), then they are comparatively easy to rebut.

However, when one has made such a 'theoretical' defence of Marxism, one has achieved something, but not very much. For the real events – the show trials, the labour camps, the disastrous twists and turns of inter-war Comintern policy, the behaviour of the Communists in Spain, 1956 in Hungary, 1968 in Czechoslovakia, and now the current events in Poland – still have to be faced, understood and their political lessons learnt. In a sense, this book is my attempt to learn them. But what I have been concerned to establish in this section is that their reality can easily be denied and their import obfuscated if they are generalized into essentially abstract, philosophical problems in 'Marxist theory'. For then it is possible to 'solve' these problems theoretically, to show that their postulation rests on misunderstanding or a 'partial' or 'particular' interpretation of Marx and to think that, this done, Marxism is somehow 'off the hook' for all these horrors in the real world. But Marxism is both a theory and a practice, or more precisely, it is a theory for practice, and it is thus responsible for both sides of its dual identity. To really come to terms with – to face – what has been done in the name of Marxism and to create a Marxism that is better in practice as well as in theory, we need to (a) understand Marx's theory as itself an historical product, and (b) analyse both the theory and practice of later Marxists concretely in their particular historical contexts,

and not in the totally misleading and un-Marxist form of
'theoretical debate'. It seems to me that on the whole
Thompson's *Poverty of Theory*, Anderson's reply,* and most of
the subsequent contributions to the debate in the *History
Workshop Journal* have been of this misleading 'theoretical'
form, and have therefore dodged the central political issues (the
issues which I think Thompson wanted to raise in *The Poverty of
Theory* but managed to obscure totally in his obsession with
'Althusserianism'). For if what we really need to talk about is
Stalin, Spain, Prague in 1968 or Poland now, let's talk about them
directly, not about 'economism', 'reductionism' or whatever.
There is something (though not very much) to be got out of the
latter. There is a very great deal to be got out of the former.

The real causes of Left intellectual élitism in Britain

I noted at the beginning of this appendix that Edward Thompson
saw a marked intellectual and political élitism as being one of the
consequences of the 'Stalinism' of the intellectual New Left in
Britain. I have argued that a Stalinist politics need not follow
from an acceptance of Marx's basic political economy and that
the real causes of Stalinism lie elsewhere. I also think, therefore,
that Thompson mistook the real underlying causes of the Left's
intellectual élitism, though he described the phenomenon and
some of its more pernicious consequences accurately enough. I
will end this appendix by offering an alternative explanation of
this élitism.

Some Marxists invite opponents to state their 'viewpoints',
knowing in advance that whatever is said, they will knock the
'viewpoint' to smithereens. And the arguer? Battered adults
may make good troops to follow a leader; they don't make a
liberation movement.**

---

* Perry Anderson, *Arguments within English Marxism*, London, Verso, 1980.
** Trevor Pateman, *Language, Truth and Politics*, Sidmouth, Pateman & Stroud,
1975, p. 45.

This quotation certainly grasps part of what is involved, i.e. the treating of argument as a 'war' or 'battle' in which the prime aim is to 'crush' an 'opponent' (or rather his or her 'position') rather than to enlighten or aid understanding. Here the starting point is an unyielding intellectual monism, i.e. the view that there is only one 'right' or 'correct' position with respect to any issue and that one is occupying that position oneself. Hence one's opponent is necessarily 'wrong' and the dominant, indeed sole aim of the argument is to demonstrate to him or her that he or she is 'wrong'. This kind of stance frequently overlooks the possibility that the 'opponent' may not be defining the 'issue' in the same way, that consequently his or her viewpoint may contain more important elements of truth about a different but related issue, etc. Above all it is predicated upon a total self-confidence in the correctness of one's own position, and so – and this is the central point – 'failure' of 'the opponent' to grasp the 'incorrect' nature of his or her counter-position (it is significant I think that as I write military analogies and language seem to present themselves naturally – they grasp also an important part of the psychology involved) can only be explained as the product of stupidity. This stupidity may consist in being unable to move beyond the parameters of some 'ideology' ('populism', 'social democracy', national or sexual 'chauvinism', etc.) or it may consist in simple illogicality (or the two may be seen to be related), but in either case the only available response is contempt, i.e. dismissal or negation of the 'opponent' who is both intellectually and personally 'written off', treated as intellectually 'hopeless', incorrigibly venal or both. And this style of argument is reinforced by gesture, by facial expressions (the sneer is omnipresent) and by tones of voice which may be as wounding or frightening in themselves as any of the content of the argument.

All this is perhaps at its most pernicious when it is combined with formal relations of power or authority either inside political sects or in teacher/student relationships in universities or elsewhere. For this style of argument both reflects and reinforces power relationships in which the teacher or leader is surrounded by a group of neophytes whose primary role is simply to echo the latest 'positions' which the leader has adopted, while the leader maintains his or her position by constant demonstrations of the 'correctness' of his or her latest formulations using the kind of techniques outlined above.

Now I do not wish this account to suggest that one is dealing here with some form of 'brainwashing'. The point is rather that certain Left intellectuals with great logical and argumentative skills and enormous self-confidence may be able to obtain disciples among people with less self-confidence by methods which rely only partly on intellectual conviction, or which, more exactly, combine intellectual persuasion with certain forms of psychological and emotional pressure which may not be entirely conscious or intended.

These observations are not new, and feminists in particular have drawn attention to these and similar techniques and have suggested that they are a reflection of the male dominance of Left activity, a form of intellectual 'machismo'. However, since I have observed not dissimilar trends among some feminists (see Chapter 4), I suggest that these patterns of behaviour have rather broader and deeper roots in the very nature of radical politics.

To take up a radical political position, in any society, is by definition to distance oneself from the mainstream beliefs and values of that society. If in addition one is attacking some of the central sustaining institutions and values of that society (private property, materialism, competitive individualism, racism, patriarchy, etc.) then one is likely to meet widespread indifference at best, or mass hostility at worst.

In such a profoundly 'marginalized' situation, individuals must by definition find sources of support and legitimation for their views and activity elsewhere than in the institutions of the society in which they are living. Self-confidence in one's own intellectual abilities (and thus in the unconventional views which one has taken up) is obviously such an alternative source of support.

This is perhaps one of the major reasons why Left and radical movements in general have always had a disproportionate representation of intellectuals in their leaderships and member-ships. For individuals of outstanding intellectual ability (who may indeed be formally attested as such even by the society which they are opposing) can counter the legitimation given to views by their majority status, by the alternative legitimation of 'theory'. In short, one's views may be unpopular, the views of a tiny minority, but they are nonetheless 'correct' because 'theory' (or even better, 'science') shows them to be so.

Now of course this view may be true either in general or in particular (i.e. popular views may actually be false and unpopular ones may actually be true), but whether true or not the fact is that a situation of political isolation can place a tremendous psychological premium on the constant 'theoretical' validation of one's views, both to oneself and to others. This in itself may in turn produce or encourage the kind of 'intellectual terrorism' which I have described, and which is such a marked feature of Left sects in general.

The link from this to Stalinism is I think fairly clear. Under intense political pressure, the view of opponents as intellectually or morally contemptible can be stretched to encompass their purging, imprisonment or even execution. For those regarded as intellectually or politically contemptible because they are 'wrong' or 'incorrect' may also be deemed worthless and expendable personally for the same reasons.

But while this kind of attitude may have potentially Stalinist implications, it would, I think, be disingenuous to see it merely as a problem of Stalinism. For the truth is that this kind of intellectual monism and élitism is a tendency which goes much further back in Marxism, certainly to Lenin and perhaps even to Marx and Engels themselves. I am conscious at this point, at the question of the origins and roots of the élitism in the Marxist tradition, of having opened a vast question on which others have commented, and which is certainly too large and complex to be adequately treated toward the end of an already lengthy appendix. But I would merely say here that whatever the personal behaviour of Marx or Engels in this regard, a Leninist or

177 / Appendix: politics, economics and intellectuals

'vanguardist' conception of the revolutionary party must have given considerable institutional buttressing to this kind of intellectual élitism.

And this brings me to a wider point. Throughout this appendix I have argued that the links between certain theoretical positions in Marxism and Stalinist politics are largely 'psychological' or 'emotional' rather than logical. In these pages on intellectual élitism I have talked constantly of the psychological pressures which lie behind this persistent tendency in Marxism.

This can be read as 'idealism' and will no doubt be read as such unless I attempt at least to disavow it. Therefore, let me be clear. I am not of course saying that we are dealing here with mere 'wrong ideas' which get into the heads of Marxists out of the air, because of their potty training or (à la Encounter) because of personal psychoses or 'inadequacies'.

On the contrary, I am arguing that psychological or emotional pressures derive from, or more exactly are an integral part of, real material situations, i.e. situations of acute political and social conflict or (in the case of socialist intellectuals in modern Britain) of acute social and political isolation. The real roots of Left intellectual élitism today and of the style of politics which it produces (which itself alienates many potential supporters and sympathizers) lie in that isolation.

And with this reflection I return, at its end, to a central theme of this book. For if intellectual élitism on the Left is itself rooted in the real material isolation of what I have called 'the ghetto', the increasing divorce of Left intellectuals from any effective political activity – then the solution to that problem, or at least the only real and lasting solution, lies not in theoretical critique but in finding a more viable and popular Left politics. Edward Thompson himself has returned very effectively to active politics through the revived CND, whilst the recent emergence of the Socialist Society indicates an awareness among many other Left intellectuals that they must, indeed, find a real political role in our society. What has been missing, however, and what is still missing, is even the outline of a Left political strategy appropriate to present conditions and holding out at least some hope of advance. I have tried to provide such an outline strategy in this book. I hope it will be thoroughly discussed and robustly criticized. But I also hope that criticism will itself be addressed to the task of getting socialists out of the ghetto. For it is only in that, in actual emergence from political isolation, that we can hope even to become better intellectuals. For it is as true of Left intellectuals today as of all other human beings in the past that 'the coincidence of the changing of circumstances and of human activity *or self-change* can be conceived and rationally understood only as revolutionary practice'.

For Product Safety Concerns and Information please contact our EU
representative GPSR@taylorandfrancis.com
Taylor & Francis Verlag GmbH, Kaufingerstraße 24, 80331 München, Germany